# A WOR DIFFER

## THE BIG GREEN POETRY MACHINE

## Norfolk & Suffolk

Edited by Claire Tupholme

First published in Great Britain in 2009 by:

YoungWriters

Young Writers
Remus House
Coltsfoot Drive
Peterborough
PE2 9JX
Telephone: 01733 890066
Website: www.youngwriters.co.uk


Book Design by Ali Smith & Tim Christian

SB ISBN 978-1-84431-969-5

# Foreword

Young Writers' A World of Difference is a showcase for our nation's most brilliant young poets to share their thoughts, hopes and fears for the planet they call home.

Young Writers was established in 1990 to nurture creativity in our children and young adults, to give them an interest in poetry and an outlet to express themselves. Seeing their work in print will encourage them to keep writing as they grow, and become our poets of tomorrow.

Selecting the poems has been challenging and immensely rewarding. The effort and imagination invested by these young writers makes their poems a pleasure to enjoy reading time and time again.

# Contents

**Charles Burrell Humanities School, Thetford**



**Cromer High School, Cromer**



**Diss High School, Diss**

### Elm Tree Middle School, Lowestoft



### Northgate High School, Ipswich



### Old Buckenham High School, Old Buckenham



### Stowmarket Middle School, Stowmarket

# The Poems

# My Best Friend Is Black

My best friend is black
But I am white
He gets teased whereas I don't
The bullies always hurt him,
Call him names I do not wish to repeat.
They sometimes come up to me and say:
Why do you hang around with a black boy,
When you are white! Loser!
I don't get it?
They call him names but not me?

When I see him getting hurt, or even laughed at!
It makes my blood run cold.
My blood bubbles up and I feel so frustrated!
I can't stop them from doing it!
That's the worst part.
I can see my friend getting hurt,
And I can't help him.

My stomach churns and I feel sick,
Bullies only hurt people
Because they have no friends
My mum said they were racist and explained it
I was so mad I felt tears welling up in my eyes,
My best friend is black
And I don't care what colour he is!

**Lily Brown (11)**
Caister High School, Caister-on-Sea

# Recycling, Recycling

Recycling, recycling that's what we need to do!
Recycling, recycling, fill up your green bins!
Recycling, recycling, reuse your plastic bags!
Recycling, recycling, don't chuck away that glass!
Recycling, recycling, compost those leftovers!
Recycling, recycling, have fun at the tip!
Recycling, recycling, that's what we need to do!

**Georgina Learmonth (11)**
Caister High School, Caister-on-Sea

# Did You See The News?

Did you see the news?
Did you see the news today?
A woman in Brixton mourning
The bullet took another son away.

Everybody is asking
The simple question why?
Why this innocent eight-year-old?
Why did he have to die?

Did you see the news?
Did you see the news today?
A woman in Brixton mourning,
The bullet took another son away.

Yet this isn't the first time,
It has happened before.
The newspapers repeating the same story,
But a different victim, one more.

Did you see the news?
Did you see the news today?
*I'm* the woman in Brixton, mourning
The bullet took *my* son away.

Why did they do it?
They were on a killing spree,
But when they pulled that stone-cold trigger,
Did they ever think of *me*?

Did you see the news
Did you see the news today?
*I'm* the woman in Brixton mourning,
The bullet took my son away.

He was so full of laughter,
He had a sunshine smile
I know hearts heal, and love lives on,
But it's going to take a while.

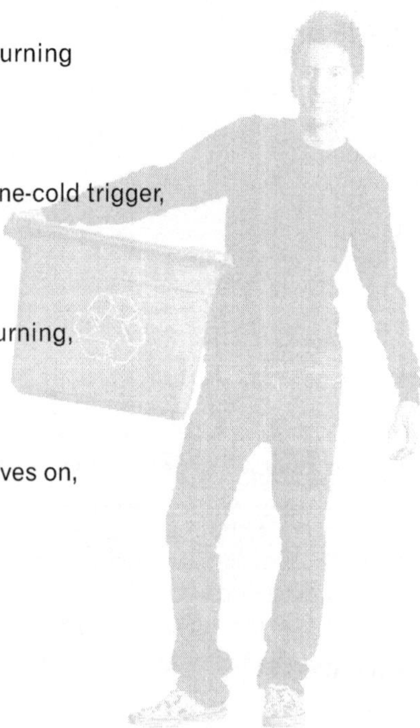

**Alexandra Cheung (12)**
Caister High School, Caister-on-Sea

# The 3 R's

Reduce, reuse, recycle
A poem to help the world out,
It could change our lives forever,
And here's what it's all about.

Reduce your carbon footprint,
To help us through this tough time,
Help us to reduce,
And everyone will be fine.

Reduce, reuse, recycle
A poem to help the world out,
It could change our lives forever,
And here's what it's all about.

Reduce all your old stuff,
Make it into something new,
It helps to save the planet,
And gives you something to do!

Reduce, reuse, recycle
A poem to help the world out,
It could change our lives forever,
And here's what it's all about.

Recycle all your old rubbish,
It's not so hard to do,
Just keep those empty bottles,
Newspaper and cardboard too!

Reduce reuse recycle
A system to help the world out,
Could change our lives forever,
And that's what it's all about.

**Lauren J K Brown (13)**
Caister High School, Caister-on-Sea

# Save The Animals

Sirens go off as more danger comes
A huge roar as more four-wheeled monsters pass
Racing the cheetahs
An uneven beat is echoing through the air
As axe meets tree
*Pow!*
*Snap!* . . .
Everything is silent
Trees fall as in slow motion
*Crash!*
Everything is chaos
Birds fly for their freedom
Small animals scatter to their nests
Everyone runs to safety
All
Except that one wolf
Searching for her pup
'Where are you' she cries
She carries on searching
Until the pup is found.

Barks then fill the air
As they charge towards her
Obeying orders from two-legged people
She struggles
She yelps
She lies next to her pup
Neither moving
Neither breathing
Save the animals!

**Bethany Youngs (12)**
Caister High School, Caister-on-Sea

# The World Today

The animal's happiness is dying
All the birds have stopped flying
All because we don't look after the world today.

The water is disappearing,
While their heart is rearing
Their loved ones are dying in distress

When it comes to pollution
There must be a solution
We need to work together to find it out.

The cars are to blame
We ride to school in shame
How do we put up with this terror?

Trees need to be planted
On flat land and slanted
To give everyone oxygen, beauty and a home.

To animals that can climb
Hurry up we don't have much time
They're dying as we speak.

We can all do our bit
So there's space for everyone to fit
Save the world today to make it OK!
For us to live in a happy environment.

**Lauren Elisabeth Murray Daniels (12)**
Caister High School, Caister-on-Sea

# It's Not Fair!

It's not fair!
What does she know about it not being fair?
She has nice clothes, nice shoes, nice hair
She has a house made of bricks and mortar
She has enough food
She has enough water
There are children starving everywhere
So what does she know about it not being fair?

**Kathryn Rose Noble (12)**
Caister High School, Caister-on-Sea

# Untitled

Why are people always wanting more?
Why are people racist?
Why do people think it's OK to abuse things?

I will tell you why this is
This world is greedy
Everyone thinks it's OK to do as they please
And everyone thinks it's funny to watch someone die.

Why do people think it's OK to smoke?
Why do they think it OK to drink?
Why do people take advantage of drugs?
I will tell you why this is
Because they think it's cool
They don't realise what it does to them
They can't take the stress so they calm with this sensation.

Why do people always take advantage of their friends?
Why do people take advantage of their family?
Why do people take advantage of their money?

I will tell you why this is
They don't realise what friends they had until they're gone.
They don't realise that families are there for help and love.
They don't realise that money is very short.

*People can be really mean!*

**Kelly Owen (13)**
Caister High School, Caister-on-Sea

# Rainforest, The Sea

I walked through the deep dark jungle,
Monkeys swinging from tree to tree,
Elephants spraying water everywhere,
But we are tearing all that apart.

Bubbles float above me as I breathe,
Seaweed as green as the grass,
Swaying around as the fishes go past,
But it won't stay that way if it gets polluted.

**Lucy Austin (11)**
Caister High School, Caister-on-Sea

# Me, However, Him!

As I cross a busy street
My eyes are drawn to ragged feet.

I stare down into a sadden face
Time stands still in this lonely place.

My coat and scarf all nice and warm
His clothes all tattered and torn.

I live in a house, which I call home
He has to make do with a cardboard dome.

As I take a seat to eat my meal
He will have to beg and steal.

As I lay snug with my quilt wrapped around
He will lay cold on the frozen ground.

I keep my friends and family near
He has no one to hold him, dear.

As I reach into my purse
Is one gold coin all he's worth?

Maybe if people cared a little more
Men like him would have their own front door.

Homeless is a place no one should be
In 2008 it's sad to see.

**Sundee Denton Chandler (12)**
Caister High School, Caister-on-Sea

# Why?

Why suffer in silence when others speak aloud
Why be upset when others are proud
Why stay up at night and think about
What they've said
You're fat, you're ugly and I wish you were dead.
Why is the question and why is all I say
So speak aloud and live your life the normal way.

Bullying - see it, stop it, tell!

**Rebecca Kemp (12)**
Caister High School, Caister-on-Sea

# Stop!

Stop the racism,
Stop the racism
Stop the racism *now!*

Stop offending others,
We're all just the same,
Yellow, black, white,
Coloured skin doesn't matter.

Don't offend others' religion,
We're all just the same,
Islamaphobia and Anti-Semitism,
Don't offend the world.

Racial segregation,
Apartheid,
We're all just the same,
Don't separate others.

Don't be against other nationalities
Don't be against others
We're all the same,
But different in our own way . . .

We're all the same
*But in a different good way!*

**Leah Smith (11)**
Caister High School, Caister-on-Sea

# Recycling!

Save more trees,
From being cut down.
Follow the green arrows,
Going around.

A worn out newspaper,
Can last forever,
Don't throw away
Think again about paper,
Reduce, reuse, recycling.

**Victoria Lowe (11)**
Caister High School, Caister-on-Sea

# Who's Poor?

What do you think makes us poor?
Is it not having the latest designer clothes?
Or being like Oliver Twist and having to ask,
'Please sir, can I have some more?'
In Britain we have all that we need,
Clothes on our backs, food, fresh water
And shoes on our feet
The extras we take for granted
And want because of our greed.
I've been to a country that is truly poor
The smiling coast of West Africa
Where even water can kill.
No shoes, no food on a table
And clothes handed down ten times or more.
We can all learn a lesson
From these families so poor.
They're never unhappy,
They're thankful for all they receive.
Not once will you hear them say
'It's not fair you must give me more!'
So people tell me who you think is poor.
These friendly happy people
Or us Britons who always want more!

**Fiona Bray (12)**
Caister High School, Caister-on-Sea

# Why Is it

Why is it mankind destroys the world
Cutting down trees, killing animals.
The world is square but curved,
Why do we pollute so much?
Leaving our rubbish behind
Keeping lights on,
Wasting electricity everyday
People are like the destroyers,
Out to kill all!

**Amy-Jane Pegler (12)**
Caister High School, Caister-on-Sea

# The Fight For Food

We can't find food,
Our country is fighting,
Our fields have landmines,
No room to grow crops.

Our government spends money,
On weapons and soldiers,
Burning our fields,
And contaminating water.

No money left
For farmers and food,
We are all hungry,
Will somebody help?

We've now left our country,
To find safety and food,
We're happy and full,
Our new life has begun.

Some of our family,
Are left in poverty,
The fight for food,
Goes on in Africa.

**Jack Southgate (11)**
Caister High School, Caister-on-Sea

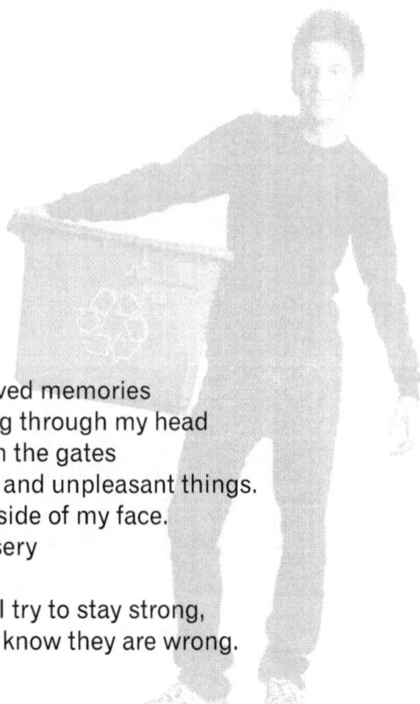

# It's Always Me!

I wake up every morning
Dreading the day ahead
As I walk to school the engraved memories
And suicidal thoughts running through my head
They stood staring at me from the gates
They started to shout coward and unpleasant things.
My silent tears ran down the side of my face.
They have made my life a misery
And have taken all my mates
They made me feel weak but I try to stay strong,
And deep in their hearts they know they are wrong.

**Samantha Hunn (12)**
Caister High School, Caister-on-Sea

# Poor Children

Poor little orphan child traipsing down the street,
Dressed in tattered clothing with nothing on his feet,
With bruises all down his neck I feel so sorry for him,
Life really isn't fair so why can't we all just share?

In Asia there is child poverty,
They're kids, can't anyone see,
Still they have to work hard for most of the day,
They have no time to be kids and run around and play.

See that child battered up the road,
The screams and shouts of the child echoed.
His body was as dirty as coal,
I feel some people have no soul.

We can help these children you know,
Support them wherever you go,
Donate some things to charity,
Go fundraising and raise some money,
Do a sponsored event.

However, heart and soul
Must be in the content.

**Hannah Gibson (11)**
Caister High School, Caister-on-Sea

# Life Is Hard

Life is hard
You could describe it as a lump of lard
In a pan ready to melt
I stick to my rules
And play it cool
Gangs and mobs taunt me every night
My mind is tired I'm not up for a fight
My shelter is a doorway, my bed is a box
My only comfort is an urban fox
Who like me has to scrounge around?
To survive this hard life in the town.
*Life is hard*!

**Callum Townsend (12)**
Caister High School, Caister-on-Sea

# Killing

Animals why?
It's the same as doing it to humans.
Stabbing, shooting, beating to death.
Humans have a right to live so do animals.

Humans why?
People doing it to impress their friends.
Their friends and family screaming for help.
Animals have a right to live so do humans.

Environment why?
People doing it without realizing
Cars, fires, chemicals and fumes destroying homes.
Everyone and everything has a right to live so does Earth.

Animals, humans, Earth
People thinking they are cool
But they're killing
Wars taking place,
Habitats getting destroyed,
Day and night
Killing isn't funny it's a crime.

**Gemma Skipper (12)**
Caister High School, Caister-on-Sea

# War

War is hard, war is scary,
War needs a magic fairy,
People dying and people crying,
Young people in their grave,
All those soldiers are so brave.

War is noisy, war is loud,
You can see the soldiers in the clouds,
War is tough,
And people live rough,
Stop the fighting and the biting,
Let's be friends
And then the war ends.

**Lucie Morris (11)**
Caister High School, Caister-on-Sea

# Extinction

They travel around wild,
Roaming free
Pouncing through the forest
Between the trees,
The poacher he waits with his loaded gun,
It'll be too late when it's all done.

The animals are becoming less and less
This problem needs to be addressed
These beautiful creatures should be saved
Stop it now rules must be obeyed.

Dinosaurs are now a thing of the past
What a shame I wish it could have last
We need to save for all to see
How magnificent these creatures could have been.

Extinction is an awful thing
Eventually it could kill everything
That's why we have to stop
But so we know when and how?

**Jack Jarvis (12)**
Caister High School, Caister-on-Sea

# It's Silly

Why do they kill? It's silly
Why not peace?
What? This about religions? It's silly
Can't you agree they believe differently?
Why fight? It's silly
Why not just make up?

Now I know why
My mummy told me
They kill
They fight
It's not right
It's silly
So why war?

**Morgan Harvey (12)**
Caister High School, Caister-on-Sea

# Thoughts Of War

War is a time, a time with no pace
And it shows no grace.
It can take away your right
To be or become
And the people at home
Think there's good being done.
But when or if it might happen to you,
You might not live to tell the gloom,
The endless beating of gunfire over your head
And feeling the dread you might lie with the dead
The desert can be a terrible place.
The only battleground to deny the right to see.
The force you may flee,
It can be a place of suffering
As if a desert of destruction,
A desert of demoralization.
The gunshots now begin to fade,
You close your eyes
And are ready for your grave.

**Nathan Grant (11)**
Caister High School, Caister-on-Sea

# What Can I See . . .

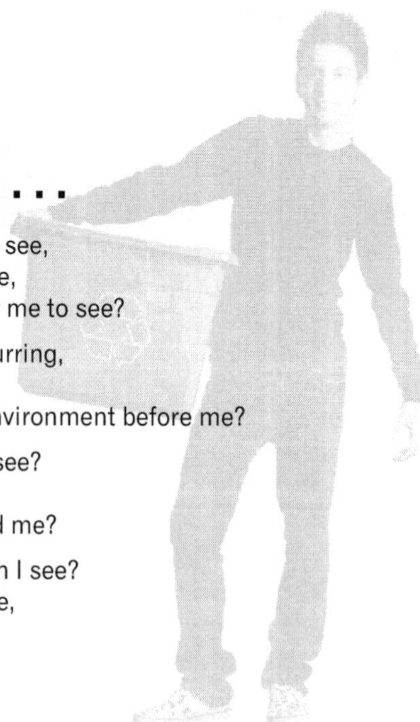

I look around with nothing to see,
No polar bears not even a tree,
Where is the environment for me to see?

Freak accidents keep on occurring,
From Katrina to the tsunami,
What has happened to the environment before me?

I look around me what can I see?
Is it winter in summer?
What is happening all around me?

I look into the future what can I see?
Reduce, recycle and FairTrade,
Is the right path for me!

**Tia Fitzgerald (12)**
Caister High School, Caister-on-Sea

# I Am Homeless

The night draws in to settle down,
I look at the sky with a frown,
My blanket is my best friend to me,
As I lay it down on a doorstep that's free,
I have no money for food or drink,
I am homeless I have no time to think.

The rain pours down, the wind does blow
Time to me goes so slow,
I wrap my blanket tightly around
As I lay down on the ground
All I want is a meal for a pound,
I am homeless I do not hear a sound.

So I shout and call out loud,
To the passing sky and clouds
It's time to act and stop this now,
Let's join together and shout out loud
To stop all homeless I stand so proud
Can you hear me? I call out loud.

**Lee Sharp (12)**
Caister High School, Caister-on-Sea

# Save Our Planet

S o much nature is dying of pollution
A nimals are nearly gone 'cause of litter
V olvos and other cars are letting fumes out
E ach and every day millions of trees are getting cut down

O ur ozone layer is about to burst
U nder the red-hot sun our plants are dying
R ead on with the poem and change your ways.

P eople are dying of unhealthy water
L isten and pay attention now
A nd take care of your planet
N ever give up or back down
E nd this pollution and
T ry your hardest to stop pollution.

**Alix Webb (12)**
Caister High School, Caister-on-Sea

# Endangered And Extinct Animals

I am a giant panda,
I used to live in a forest
But now
It is gone.

I am a polar bear
All fur and fluff
That's what humans
Like about me!

I am a tiger
Known as a scavenger
I'm killed for my coat
By poachers alike.

With every cruel footstep
We are watching
Watching you
Why? why? why?
We want to live.

**Chloe Brown (11)**
Caister High School, Caister-on-Sea

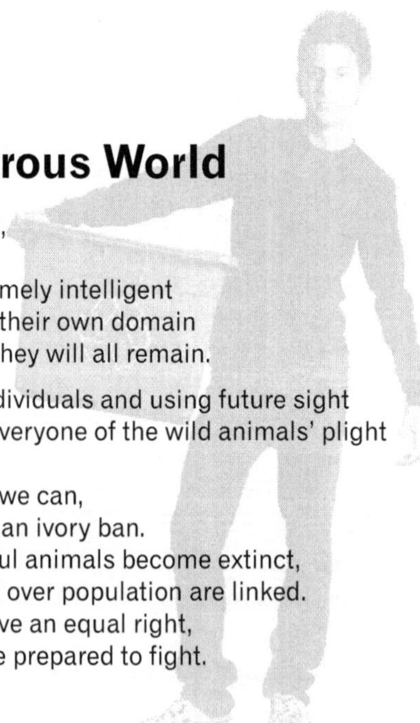

# Save Our Wondrous World

Wild animals are magnificent,
Powerful and heaven-sent
Untamed, beautiful and extremely intelligent
Master of their own habitats, their own domain
I hope for centuries to come they will all remain.

As young, caring, growing individuals and using future sight
At every opportunity inform everyone of the wild animals' plight
We must avoid wasting
The planet's resources when we can,
Do not wear fur and insist on an ivory ban.
Ensure that no more wonderful animals become extinct,
That destroying our trees and over population are linked.
That animals and humans have an equal right,
And against all opposition are prepared to fight.

**Chloe Jarvis (11)**
Caister High School, Caister-on-Sea

## Homeless People

As I walk the streets alone
I wish I had a place to call my own
I hate it at night as it is so cold
I feel it more because I am old
I am in pain
From others' gain
No one understands how it feels
Not to have any meals
I wish I had a bed
To rest my swollen head
I have bruises and cuts from where people hit me
Because I am homeless and smell of pee
My poor dead wife
Took her own life
She left me alone
I needed a big loan
Now look where I am
*Homeless.*

**Ashlea Clark (12)**
Caister High School, Caister-on-Sea

## Animal Cruelty

A nimals
N eed
I nstinct when their
M others go
A way and
L eave them.

C hildren need to
R ealise and
U nderstand the
E ffect it has on the
L ives of
T he
Y oung baby animals.
*Don't kill them*!

**Ryan Labrum (11)**
Caister High School, Caister-on-Sea

# The World is Wasting

The world is wasting, wasting away
The world is wasting, wasting today
But to who?
Is it wasting because of me or you?
When the trees are cut down
Does it really make us frown?
Or does it just pass by us?
Well after all what is all the fuss?
If we cut down on $C0_2$
Would it really make our rivers flow?
Would our world be better if we stopped the wars
And put in some more laws?
If we're wasting energy
We're wasting money
Come on people of the world
This isn't funny
It's so simple to save on energy we use
In fact all we need to do is recycle or reuse.

**Lucy Bentley (12)**
Caister High School, Caister-on-Sea

# Going Green

When people drop their litter
It doesn't look like glitter
I try not to feel bitter
When I see people drop their litter
Rubbish attracts rats!
They scare away the cats.
I would like to sort this out
Do we have to scream?
Stop this mess, we can all try our best
Then we wouldn't get mice,
It's not very nice.
If we all go green rubbish wouldn't be seen
We don't have to be mean,
Because it would all be clean!

**Enuna Salmon (11)**
Caister High School, Caister-on-Sea

# Why?

Why are the trees being cut down?
Why are the houses pulled down?
Why oh why can't we leave them be
For all the animals and you and me.
Why do we have a war?
Why can't we take anymore
With all the sadness and pain
And people do it again and again.
With all of the poverty, racism and more
We shouldn't keep having a war.
The world would be a better place
If all of this would go away.

The poem makes me feel sad
Because we shouldn't be seeing
Poverty or war
It would make me happy if it
*Stopped!*

**Abbie Ellett (11)**
Caister High School, Caister-on-Sea

# Why Fight?

Why fight?
When you can talk,
Why fight?
When we complain it costs so much
To equip soldiers
Why fight?
When we fight for land and religion
Why not debate, get along
Or halve the land.
Why fight?
When men have accomplished
Their points without war
Why fight?
Answer me one question
What does war accomplish?

**Billy Peace (11)**
Caister High School, Caister-on-Sea

# So what's The Point?

Rainforests are green but
Some people are keen
To cut down the rainforest
So animals are not seen.

Others disagree
And want there to be
A rainforest for people
To enjoy and see.

So what's the point?
In cutting it down
It will upset the people
And make the animals frown.

So tell me
Is it right or is it wrong
To cut down the rainforest
Where the animals belong?

**Eleanor Randall (11)**
Caister High School, Caister-on-Sea

# Stabbing

I'm gonna get stabbed,
Me and my gang
We hit him, we kicked him
The gun went bang
I dropped dead
Because I got shot in the head
I wish I could switch my life
But I got stabbed
I wish I could switch my life
But it's too late
I got stabbed
There are too many stabbings today
We should have got rid of it yesterday
And if you stab
You'll get stabbed.

**Sam Gordon (12)**
Caister High School, Caister-on-Sea

# Why Me?

I cry because I am in pain
Everyone laughs, sneers and calls me insane
They think they're so big
They threaten to hit me with a twig.

I'm in so much fear
When you are near
You think I'm your slave
I'm so sad I might as well dig a grave.

You call me names
I'm sick of all your games
Who are you to pick me apart?
I'm not a board for your dart.

I want to be happy, to never frown
My watery tears in what I will drown
Beating myself up over fright
Crying myself to sleep at night.

**Ellie Salmon (12)**
Caister High School, Caister-on-Sea

# Mad Strange World

The world is strange!
The world is mad!
People are happy!
People are sad!
The man on the corner smoking a fag,
His life he carries in a plastic bag,
The man in his Porsche with his designer wife,
We all want his kind of life.
The drunk on the bench begging for change,
Why is the world becoming so strange?
But who is happy?
Who is sad?
The world is strange!
The world is mad!

**Robbie Witney (12)**
Caister High School, Caister-on-Sea

# Let's

Let's ride our bikes to school today,
Breathe in the cool fresh air.
Let's leave the car at home today,
Feel the wind blow through our hair.

Let's take our bottles to be recycled,
Don't throw them in the bin.
You know we'll get a good feeling,
When we help the world to win.

Let's pick our strawberries from the field,
Not flown in from abroad.
Let's eat a few while we pick,
Will that make me a fraud?

Let's turn off our lights when we go out,
We can save energy.
Let's save the power for the world,
And live in harmony.

**Thomas Bensly (12)**
Caister High School, Caister-on-Sea

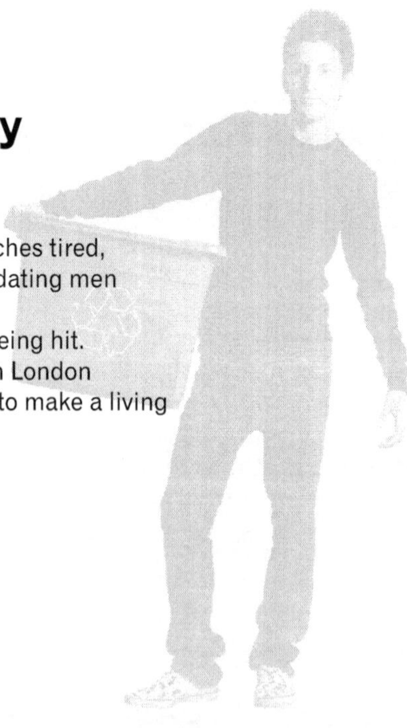

# War And Poverty

Disbelief is always there
Lurking round the corner,
Terrified men hide in the trenches tired,
In the distance insane, intimidating men
Shoot in all directions.
There is always a chance of being hit.
At the same time in a street in London
A poor man desperately tries to make a living
He begs for money,
But people just walk past
As if no one is there,
The men in the trenches,
The men on the floor,
All realise life is poor.

**Simeon Cookson (12)**
Caister High School, Caister-on-Sea

# I Once Had A Dream

I once had a dream . . .
No wars just love, peace and happiness
Food and clothing for all
And plenty for the poor
That thou shall not be prejudiced or disrespectful.

I once had a dream . . .
That we will be free
That we will be risen above the crowd
That we will be accepted
That we will be kind to one another.

I once had a dream . . .
We will share the rights to be responsible
We will stop cutting down habitats
We will stop ruining humans homes
We will stop the pollution.

I once had a dream . . .

**May Speck (11)**
Caister High School, Caister-on-Sea

# A Green Mind

Our animals are dying
Soon they'll be rare
Big business earns millions
But doesn't care
Rivers all full of chemicals
Choking the fish
Air full of fumes
Against our wish.
Recycling is a part
We can all play,
Saving energy
Is something we can do today.
To preserve the future of mankind,
We all have to think with a green mind.

**Shanice Simmonds (11)**
Caister High School, Caister-on-Sea

# The Rainforest

I walked to the edge of the rainforest
I heard a buzz in my ears,
I thought it was a mosquito,
But then I heard the word *timber*
Shouted out loud,
And a tree came crashing down,
Too close for comfort.
There were giant machines,
Clearing large parts of the forest
And spilling pollution everywhere.
Native people and animals,
Losing their natural habitats
And ways of life,
Forcing the people to live in the cities and in poverty
And animals and plants to disappear forever.
Come on start reusing, recycling,
Get a grip man, this is our *world!*

**Jamie Himpleman (12)**
Caister High School, Caister-on-Sea

# War!

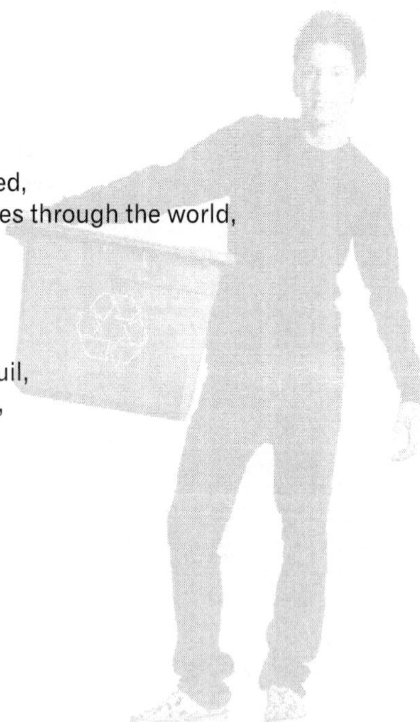

The diminutive minds of hatred,
Enraged heads as anger passes through the world,
Although victims grieve
Killers rage on,
Mad or just stupid,
Peace, they may say,
Although peace means tranquil,
People dying is not calmness,
Just selfishness,
They want it their own way!
Way?
For greed or money?
I ask for discontinuation,
I ask for real peace.

**Tom McGee (12)**
Caister High School, Caister-on-Sea

# Emotions

Darkness
Fear!
Excitement
Noise
Hush
Then cries
What's going on above us
In those war torn skies?
Fright
Alarm
And panic
As the bombs seem to come our way
Then joy
Relief
Happiness
Knowing safety's here to stay.

**Harry Stannard (12)**
Caister High School, Caister-on-Sea

# Just Look Around

Look around at the people you see.
What do you feel
When you walk past the homeless on the street?
What stares back at you
When you look in the mirror?
How can we all sleep,
When half the world weeps?

A mother will need to find shelter for tonight.
They're going to try and build their house tonight
And that kid will have to go through the bins
To find food tonight.

But with a click of our fingers
We could change the world in which we live
Look at the people you see
So now what do you feel?

**Hayley Champion (12)**
Caister High School, Caister-on-Sea

# Extinction

It's wet and hot,
Do we give a jot?
Some of us do
Some of us don't
Should we care
What's in the air?

Where have all the animals gone?
They disappeared just after that bomb,
What about the litter we throw away?
I'll pick it up another day,
You are black and I am white,
I really - don't want to fight.

It's time to stop and think,
Before our world is on the brink,
. . . of destruction.

**Patrick Edwards (12)**
Caister High School, Caister-on-Sea

# Happy People

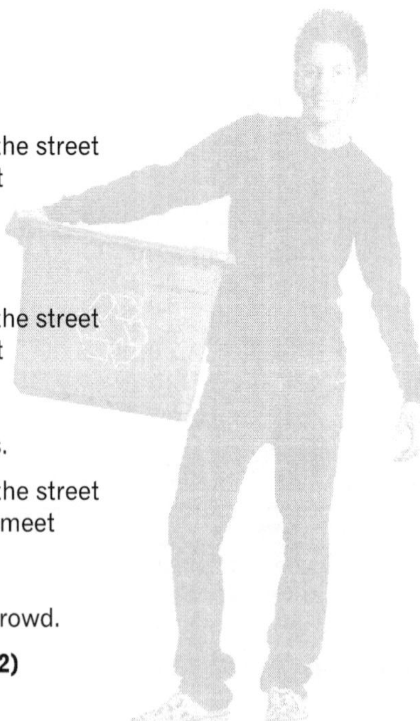

Happy people walking down the street
Talking to everyone they meet
Shaking hands
Smiling faces
Carrying all their suitcases.

Happy people walking down the street
Talking to everyone they meet
Waving hands
Laughing faces
Still carrying all the suitcases.

Happy people walking down the street
Laughing with everyone they meet
Waving hands
Laughing out loud
Mixing with everyone in the crowd.

**Kimberlea Joy Stedeford (12)**
Caister High School, Caister-on-Sea

# Danger Or Peace?

Millions of people live in a world full of attacks,
A world full of greedy and selfish people
That just hate peace
I keep hearing the radio talk out some very sad news.
Everyone should have the right to be happy and sheltered,
Not to be attacked by other people.

No matter if you're rich, poor, old, young
We all have the right to be free
Like birds up in the sky and
I hope the world stays like that . . .

So let's show some peace on planet Earth,
Because all of Earth prefer peace more than war,
So let's make this a dream come true.

**Lara Carlos (11)**
Caister High School, Caister-on-Sea

# Snow Leopard

Silent but deadly the snow leopard
Is a shy lonesome hunter
Razor sharp fangs and claws like steel
It lives
In the ice glazed mountains of the Himalayas
Its layers of fur keep it at a suitable temperature
While snuggled up in its cave!
Numbers dying out, this species is dying out
It will be a great loss to the animal race
To lose such an amazing animal
Years ago there were hundreds of thousands
Today just a few thousand
We need to help this animal *now*!

**Lucy Huxtable (11)**
Caister High School, Caister-on-Sea

# Trouble With Litter

Have you ever sat and wondered
What the world would be like,
If the world was full of litter
All piled up in a dyke?
Some people treat it
As if it's a bin
But it's nothing like that,
It's a planet we live in,
I know you don't think about it all of the time,
But if we all used bins
It will all be fine
So if everyone decided to do what's best
The world won't end up in a great big mess.

**Paris Taylor (12)**
Caister High School, Caister-on-Sea

# Save Our Planet

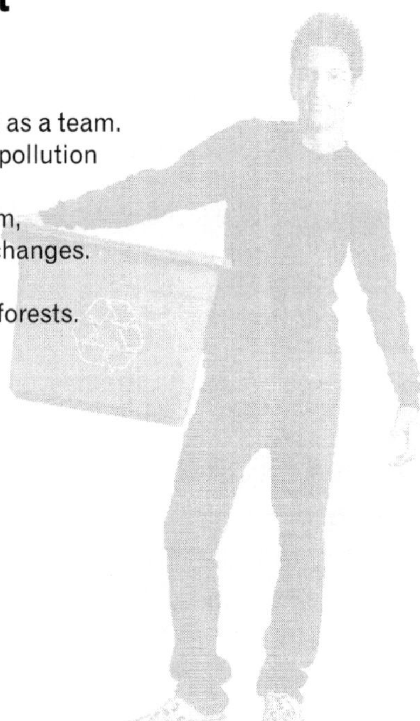

Some of the world is green
With boil and steam
We should all be keen to work as a team.
The rest of the world is full of pollution
This comes in many ways,
Homelessness, war and racism,
It can be stopped by making changes.
Recycling our litter and
Saving the world and our rainforests.
We all work together
Through all kinds of weather
And we all save the world
*All together!*

**Zoe Larner (12)**
Caister High School, Caister-on-Sea

# World

The world should be a better place
Gun, warship, war
The world should make a fresh start
Cars prevent pollution
Cars are made for motion.
The ocean is full of oil
Save the animals
Before they cry and die
People destroy the world
Keep it, save it, help it.
Help the world
People come, people go
Save the world before it goes.

**Ceri Jane Thurtle (12)**
Caister High School, Caister-on-Sea

# Bullying

Why bully it's not kind,
It's only messing with the victim's mind.
Why bully, it's a disgrace,
You're not cool, for messing someone's face.

Why bully you're not cool,
It makes you the coward or fool,
Why doesn't everyone stop rooting
And quit bullying.

If you bully
You're not clever
If we all join forces
We'll beat them together.

**Devon Troy Smith (11)**
Caister High School, Caister-on-Sea

# Racism

Great Britain is one nation,
There is no place for discrimination
People are different
Yes they are black, white, fat, thin
They shouldn't be treated like that.

Why do they do it?
It's really not fair
They are all equal to you
So, treat them with care.

Racist people are a disgrace
There is no room for them
In our human race.

**Laura Beales (12)**
Caister High School, Caister-on-Sea

# Far Within The Ancient Wood

Far within the ancient wood,
Trees laying down where they once stood.
A chainsaw that the trees had found,
Left many lay upon the ground.

For many years this carries on,
They cut them down until they're gone.
Scraping the bark all off the tree,
Why so much? It sickens me.

Far within the ancient wood,
Trees laying down where they once stood.
A chainsaw that the trees had found,
Left many lay upon the ground.

**Melissa Huggins (11)**
Caister High School, Caister-on-Sea

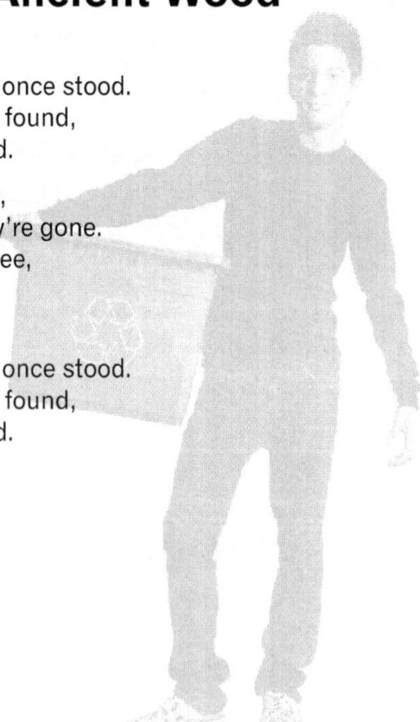

# The Servant Of The Streets

From within the shattered buildings
Or inside abandoned cars
All you can do is sit here
And stare at the night sky's stars.

Around a burning barrel
In your sleeping bag scrunched up tight
All the drunken men around you
Always looking for a fight.

People staring at you
Making such a fuss
Just get up off your feet old chap
And come and stay with us.

**Neil Green (12)**
Caister High School, Caister-on-Sea

# The Bin

I am a bin.
A lonely bin.
I stand here all day and no one
*No one,*
Puts their rubbish in me.

I am a bin.
A sad bin
No one ever gives me a second glance
And doesn't even bother with me.

I am a bin.
A bin that needs litter.
*Can you please put your litter in me?*

**Rachael Graham (12)**
Caister High School, Caister-on-Sea

# Animals In A Living Hell

As I grow up all I see
Are loads of animals needing me
Some need a home and some need food
I wish people would change their mood.

It's not their fault they are dying
I've promised myself that I'll keep trying
To help to feed them and keep them well
And save them from a living hell.

So as I get old I hope to see
A planet that lets animals be
Free and happy with nothing to fear
Year after year after year after year.

**Lloyd Daniels (11)**
Caister High School, Caister-on-Sea

# The Greatest Day For Britain

World War I full of guns,
Often not for fun
Run out of weapons, completely gone;
Lost millions but only left with one,
Done with fighting, some of them.

World War II far from over
After fighting nothing in Dover;
Run out of soldiers so they can't come home
Once, Flanders Field full of the dead,
Now full of poppy heads;
End of the war, peace has begun,
And all of our soldiers have won.

**Matthew Bailey (12)**
Caister High School, Caister-on-Sea

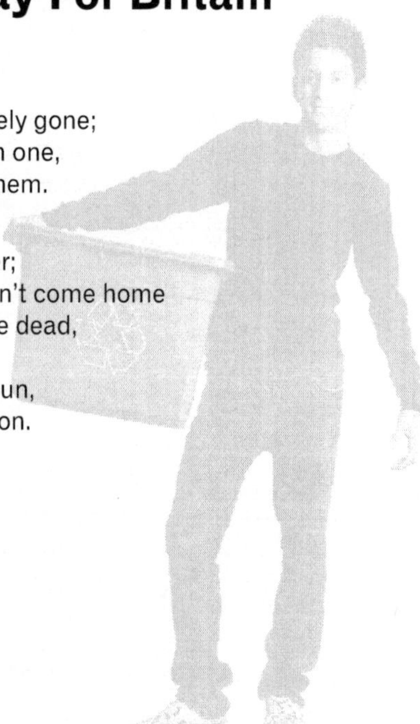

# Loneliness Of A Soldier!

I walk down a dreary street,
The rats squabble at my feet,
Children hushed in their mothers arms of protection.

Heavy armour, heavy hat.
Heavy rifle in my hand.
I listen and look for signs of bombardment and torture.

The war, the hate,
Think about home, family and mates.

Where peace and love,
This is not a war of religion and beliefs,
But a war for power.

**Taylor Seabrook (11)**
Caister High School, Caister-on-Sea

# Think How The Victim Feels

I feel diminutive
Everywhere I go I am in danger
Frightened from the other end of the room
Think how the victim feels.

Bullies are nasty for no reason at all
Why can't they treat people with respect?
Racist and aggressive
Think how the victim feels.

Deliberately picking on me
Taking their anger out
That's how the victim feels.

**Katherine Huggins (12)**
Caister High School, Caister-on-Sea

# War

Children crying,
People dying,
Bang, bang,
Shoot, shoot
Someone has to prosecute,
People plead and some bleed,
Please, please stop this war.

We need to get everything
Cleared up and done
And stick together as a team,
Let us shine like a beam.

**Joanna Zachariades (11)**
Caister High School, Caister-on-Sea

# Bully

I am strong,
He is weak as I threaten them,
I've got power,
I use abusive language against them,
It makes me feel good inside.

I am scared,
The harmful words terrorise my confidence,
It makes me feel tiny like a pea and unwanted,
Everyday I just want to hide away
So I don't want to hear the hurtful words,
I just want to curl up and die.

**Hope Brown (13)**
Caister High School, Caister-on-Sea

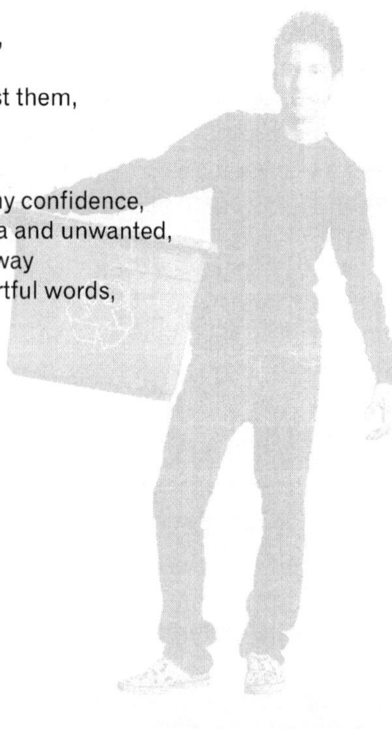

# Around The World

The rainforests must stay alive,
Pollution is killing.
Nothing will survive
Something needs to be done
Before it is too late.
Animals will die
They won't be seen again
I think this is a shame.
War is all around us
Why can't we have peace?
The world should be a better place.

**Mercedes Mayer-Henderson (12)**
Caister High School, Caister-on-Sea

# Why Have War!

The blood, guts and gore,
Against the rich and the poor,
People begging for more,
Why do we have war?
Why can't there be peace in the world?
Instead of abuse being hurled,
Let's all be safe,
Instead of armies on the case,
So let's all stop this now for the world
Or otherwise it will just be,
One big ball of terror and turmoil.

**Megan Stavaru (12)**
Caister High School, Caister-on-Sea

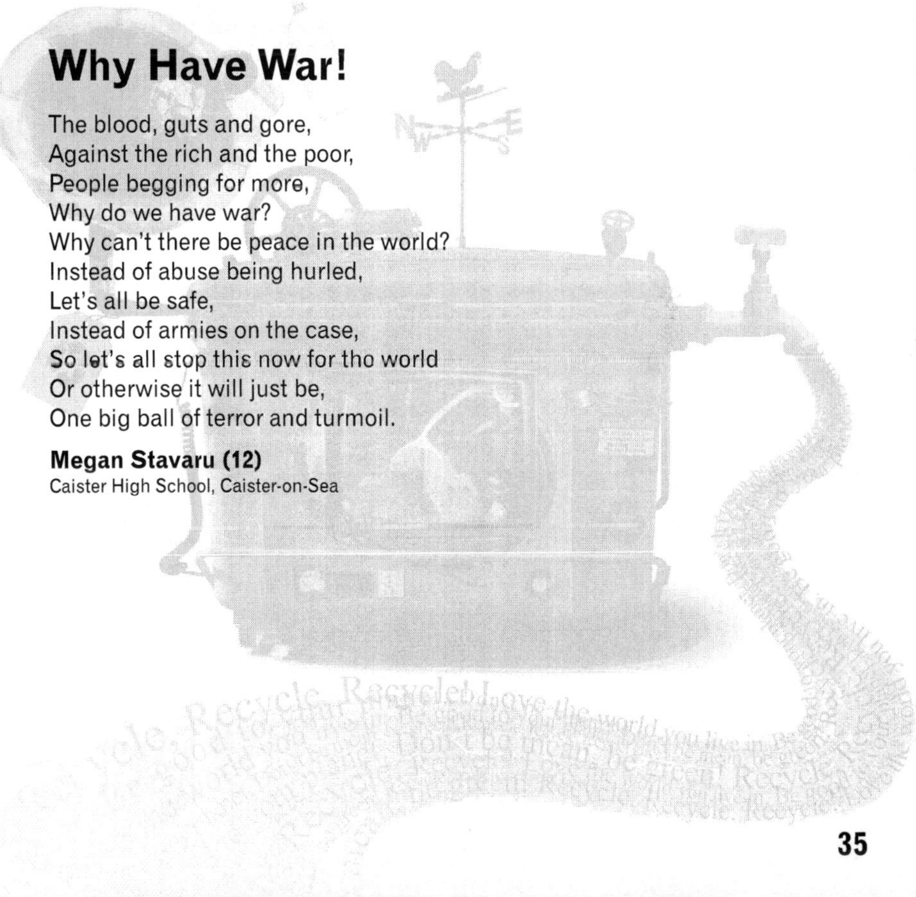

# Untitled

The hatred on one another,
The fighting and dismay,
Such horror on one girl's face,
As she sees her family and friends shot.

Bloodstained carpets,
Dead people in roads,
The men in war who have killed,
They're forever scarred.

Whoever won this war is lucky,
Yes but who suffered?

**Charlotte Warren (12)**
Caister High School, Caister-on-Sea

# Stop!

Stop starting wars
It's killing people so stop
It's scaring kids so stop.

Stop all the shooting
Stop all fighting
'Cause it's scaring people.

There would be no shelters
Or hiding
Stop the war
Then the world would be a better place.

**Daniel Marshall (12)**
Caister High School, Caister-on-Sea

# Pollution Stop

We lose people all the time,
But people will not give a dime.

Help! me here we have to stay green,
Stop, help and don't be mean.

Put your paper in a recycle bin,
Give and live, recycle that tin.

Don't throw your rubbish away,
Then your grandchildren can live and play.

*Stop! Think! Recycle! Now!*

**Jordan Tew (12)**
Caister High School, Caister-on-Sea

# Litter

When you go outside and you have got plenty of food
When you have finished make sure you are good
Don't put it on the floor,
Don't put it on the door,

When it's a windy day,
Keep your litter at bay
Make sure when put in the bin
It doesn't blow out and around again
You won't feel bltter
Because you don't drop litter.

**Melissa Aylward (13)**
Caister High School, Caister-on-Sea

# Poverty

Poor, bankrupt, broke.
Many words describe poverty,
Some get hassled a lot
And their money dwindles down
Some lay lifeless they can't
Afford to keep themselves alive.

The poor homeless people,
Wish they could dive into money
But they can't
They have nothing.

**Daniel Rawling (12)**
Caister High School, Caister-on-Sea

# War!

War!
What does it accomplish?
Sorrow, pain, death and heartbreak
Four of the worst experiences in the world
This is all war can do for you!

Loved ones and dear ones
They all come to the same end
Hope is destroyed
Fear is created
War!

**Ross Gill (11)**
Caister High School, Caister-on-Sea

# Pollution

Is there any solution to the world's pollution?
Are we really doing enough?

The world's a big place and besides the human race
Animals are finding it tough.

Polar bears are dying, we don't see them crying
But just like us they feel fear and pain.

We must keep this on our mind to the world
We must be so kind so Man and animals
Don't suffer again and again.

**Demi Taylor (12)**
Caister High School, Caister-on-Sea

# Rainforest

So colourful, so bright
Why is nothing going right?
I see people here and there
Culling trees down everywhere
Monkeys swing from tree to tree
Is anyone listening to me?
Animals losing habitats
There is something wrong with that
Stop this nonsense, stop it now
Save the rainforest today.

**Danielle Goodge (11)**
Caister High School, Caister-on-Sea

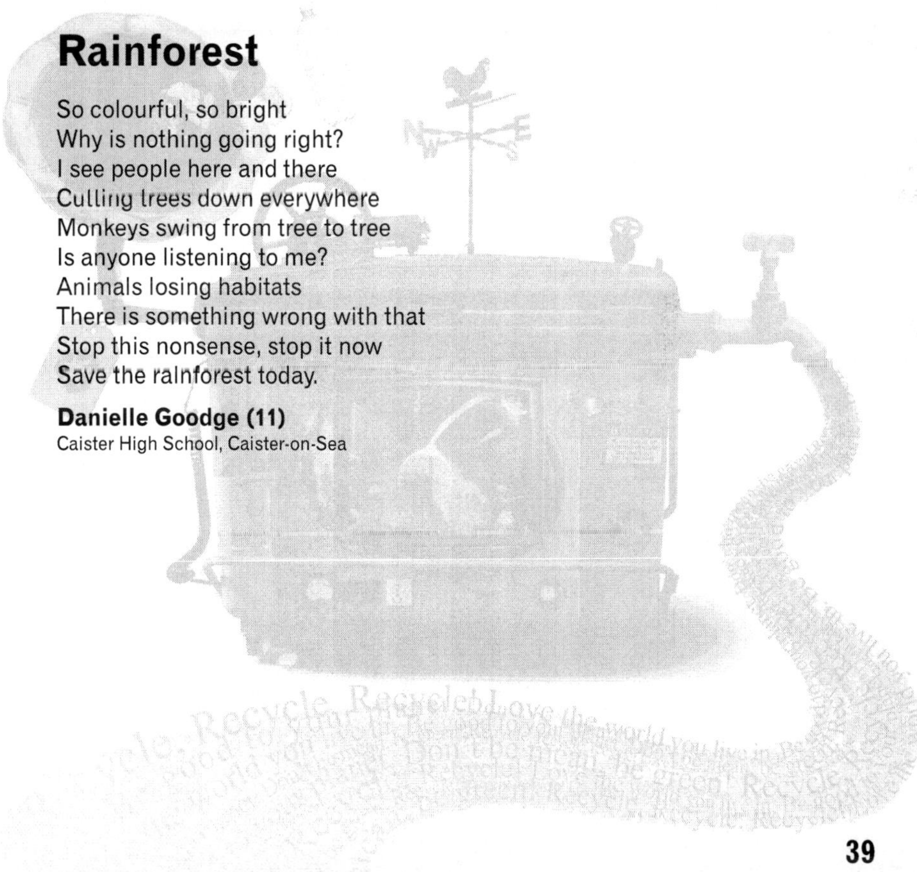

# Stop The War

*Bang!* bombs dropping.
*Swish!* planes flying.
*Argh!* people screaming
Stop the war!
Make peace to the world
Then bang! silence
No more war.
Smoke coming everywhere.
Peace, now silence
No more life.

**Connor Delaney (12)**
Caister High School, Caister-on-Sea

# War

War, war a terrible fight
No one wins, no one loses
A fight for eternity
Till the end of civilization
No one can resolve the long lasting fight
England vs Germany
Iran vs Iraq
The war never finishes
The spirit always dies
War, war.

**Garry Berger (11)**
Caister High School, Caister-on-Sea

# Poor Little Tramp

Poor little tramp on the cold street
Laying there with nothing to eat.
No money for nothing
Looking through the scrap heap
Trying to find a stroke of luck
Laying there with nothing to eat.
No house, no family
No shower for yonks
Stinking the cold night away.
That poor little tramp . . .

**Lee Roots (13)**
Caister High School, Caister-on-Sea

# Green Is The Colour

*(Inspired by Blue Is The Colour)*

Green is the colour
Recycling is the game
We need to work together
Saving our planet is our aim.

Green is the colour
Pollution needs to end
Help us to save the planet
Don't let this be the end.

**Chloe Morris (11)**
Caister High School, Caister-on-Sea

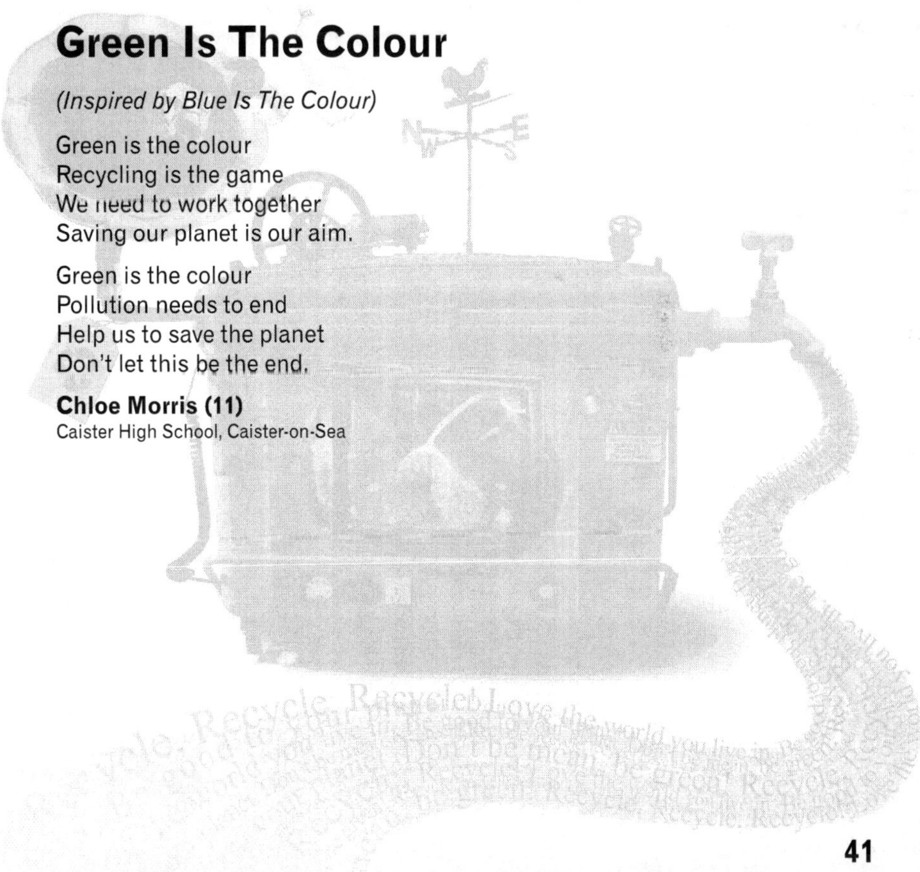

# War

*Bang, bang*
A man dying
Suffering in pain,
No help
Nothing.

A man dying
No help, no mercy
His life over.

Life is unfair!

**Jack Utting (11)**
Caister High School, Caister-on-Sea

# War

War, war
Terrible, terrible,
Think of those kids in Iraq
Losing their parents
Or losing their lives
Killing, killing, killing,
Lives going every day,
Bombs going every day,
Try to stop this.

**Jack Robert Moyse (11)**
Caister High School, Caister-on-Sea

# Littering

Litter picker
Paper chucker
Can crusher
Bag reuser
Fly tipper
*Bag It!*
*Bin it!*

**Ashley Springall (12)**
Caister High School, Caister-on-Sea

# Terrorism

T errorism needs to stop
E veryday people die
R aging madmen shooting and bombing
R evenge they say, but what for?
O ver-zealous fanatics
R eaching out across the world
I n the name of religion they claim
S hocking tactics they use
M aking the world a dangerous place.

**Callum Beales (11)**
Caister High School, Caister-on-Sea

# Racism

Everyone is a different individual
And yes we do know that.
Whether someone is silly
Or they choose to be alone
Or even if they wear a hat!
There are different colours of people
Just like a rainbow
Racism is a bad thing
And that we all should know.

**Hayley Speck (12)**
Caister High School, Caister-on-Sea

# The Rainforest

The rainforest is green
With big crisp leaves on trees
The rivers are blue and the fish are golden
The birds are singing and the leaves are rustling
The monkeys are swinging from tree to tree
The rainforest is a big home
I wish it could be my own.

**Shannon Lingwood (11)**
Caister High School, Caister-on-Sea

# Recycling, It's Endless

Recycle, recycle, recycle,
The possibilities are endless,
Reuse, reuse, reuse,
Make less waste,
Reduce, reduce, reduce,
It obviously makes sense,
Let's all go green,
It's fun for everyone,
Green, green, *go green!*

**Saphire Pettengell (12)**
Caister High School, Caister-on-Sea

# Pollution

P eople can reduce pollution
O nly helps when everyone tries
L eave the car at home
L iftshare to reduce pollution
U nderstand pollution
T ake responsibility for your carbon footprint
I ndividuals can make a difference
O ur outcome is saving our world
N othing can stop us when we work together.

**Jay Pointer (12)**
Caister High School, Caister-on-Sea

# Disappearing Rainforest

There are trees disappearing every second
Falling down every second.
Diggers destroying animal's habitats
Diggers decreasing the world's oxygen
There will be no more trees,
There will be no more animals
Soon there will be no more life!

**Ainsley Eagle (11)**
Caister High School, Caister-on-Sea

# Bullying

Is it my hair, my size or shoes?
Whatever it is I always lose
School years are long and they're supposed to be fun
This seems like a battle that can never be won.
I wish I could tell the bullies in my school,
Can you be kind and not so cruel?
Give me a chance so you can see,
There is nothing strange about me.

**Kasie Fennell (12)**
Caister High School, Caister-on-Sea

# Litter

The world would be a better place,
If only people put their litter in the right place
There's a place for plastic a place for glass,
There's a place for everything if only we asked.
God asked us to look after the world,
To do what we can, to help when it's needed
So tidy up after each other,
It's a step to what's needed.

**Olivia Hudson (12)**
Caister High School, Caister-on-Sea

# Homeless

H ungry and heartbroken
O utside with yourself or with others
M iserable and moaning for help
E ndless pain in the coldest of nights
L ost but found, on open streets
E mpty inside and . . .
S tranded alone
S orrow and sad without a home!

**Jadine Smith (11)**
Caister High School, Caister-on-Sea

# Poverty

Starving children
Having to walk miles just to get water
Think of them now
Alone in the darkness
They don't eat
Don't drink proper clean water
Think how lucky you are
Why can't everyone be treated the same?

**Chelsie Hurren (12)**
Caister High School, Caister-on-Sea

# The Polluted World

Pollution, pollution everywhere.
London, Texas even Delaware
All you see is gum and packets
All coming from people's pockets
High and low, left to right
Man, it's an awful sight
Instead of dropping all your cups
Get off your butt and pick it up.

**Curtis Trenerry (11)**
Caister High School, Caister-on-Sea

# What Am I?

I eat out of a bin,
I sit on a box,
I beg for money,
I live on the streets,
I drink out of drains,
And I have no nice clothes.
What am I?
*A hobo*

**Liam Brown (12)**
Caister High School, Caister-on-Sea

# The War

Soldiers lay in a puddle of blood,
Most have children, all are loved,
Trust nobody, that's what they were told,
No they're left out in the cold,
Was there a purpose to this cruel sacrifice?
Evidence that war is no more than a game,
That if played once, will never be played again.

**Robin Beales (12)**
Caister High School, Caister-on-Sea

# Litter

L itter is all around
I n our homes and towns
T o keep our homes neat
T idying up is a treat
E ach and every day
R ecycling is the way.

**Bradley Cruddas (11)**
Caister High School, Caister-on-Sea

# Pollution

A big problem in our world.
Pollution and global warming
Recycle and protect,
The animals have suffered enough
So when you're taking out your rubbish
Stop and think before you do.

**Megan Horsewood (11)**
Caister High School, Caister-on-Sea

# Green, Green Eco-team

Clear up the rubbish
Clean up the streets
Come jump in and clean the space
If the space is full of rubbish
Make sure there is not a trace
Stop littering and be cool.

**Sharna Bensley (11)**
Caister High School, Caister-on-Sea

# Pollution

Oh pollution,
Oh pollution everywhere
Oh how did you get there?
Rubbish why are you destroying our world?
People of the world,
Clean up the world.

**Daniel Biggs (11)**
Caister High School, Caister-on-Sea

# Recycling This And That

Recycle this
Recycle that
Even recycle your old black hat
When you recycle your old black hat
You will be purring like a well-loved cat.

**Millie Brooks (12)**
Caister High School, Caister-on-Sea

# War Into Love

War is like acid melting through our world,
Something to be forgotten and left in the past.
Love is like a locket, a locket full of hearts.
Never to be forgotten so let's make it last.

**Alisha Ruff (12)**
Caister High School, Caister-on-Sea

# No Point In War!

Millions of people die because of wars,
Millions of pounds spent on wars,
But only one disagreement starts one.

**Luke Smith (11)**
Caister High School, Caister-on-Sea

# War

W orld is at war
A nd soldiers dying
R aging soldiers doing their all.

**David Garner (13)**
Caister High School, Caister-on-Sea

# Pollution

People shouldn't throw rubbish on the floor.
People shouldn't pollute the sea.
This is the cause of global warming.
When people go to the toilet
It leads to the sea where people swim.

**Rosey Depaynville (13)**
Charles Burrell Humanities School, Thetford

# Our Little Home On The Street

Living on the streets
Afraid and alone
Nowhere to run to
Nowhere to go.

The feeling of loneliness
Cuddling to keep warm
Stomachs gurgling
Clothes torn.

Water's very little
Food even less
Struggling to survive
Lives in a mess.

Longing for somewhere
To stay for the night
But what can be done?
There is no place in sight.

People hurry past
Looking at their feet
Just trying not to disturb
Out little home on the street.

**Isabelle Trayton (13)**
Charles Burrell Humanities School, Thetford

# Say No

Say no to children
Crying
(say no)
say no to poverty
and crime
(say no)
say no to pollution
there has to be another
solution (say no)
say no to lie after lie
say no!

**Frederick Lee James Hance (12)**
Charles Burrell Humanities School, Thetford

# Make The World A Better Place!

Sun is black
Water is black
World is black
How can we save the world?

Sun should be yellow
Water should be blue
World should be happy
So everyone can smile.

People have frozen hearts
Animals have frozen hearts
Everyone is frozen
Nothing is moving around.

People should be full of love
Animals should be happy now
Everyone should walk around
Everything is moving now.

Look at rubbish on the floor
Look the homeless on the floor
Now the rubbish all picked up
Now the homeless live clean now.

**Juliya Aleskevica (13)**
Charles Burrell Humanities School, Thetford

# World Pollution

Trees' leaves can be green,
They can be kinda red
But if you keep going on like this
They'll all be dead
Icebergs are falling down, sounds like a thud,
Because of global warming we could all be in a flood
We are causing greenhouse gas,
Which goes into space in a great big mass
We don't want the water and the people to clash,
Well then let's get together and recycle our trash.

**Wesley Main (13)**
Charles Burrell Humanities School, Thetford

# Oh How The World Has Changed

Life is a creation, a gift
Being born into this world
Was the best gift a parent could give
A world with lush green fields and blue skies
With not a single cloud
Blue rivers and seas and wildlife everywhere
Where everyone was helpful and kind
But now there are no more blue seas or rivers
As they have been taken over by rubbish
The fields are taken over by house after house after house
There are now loads of clouds, clouds of pollution
The wildlife is being killed off
By people dumping their rubbish in their habitats
The streets are not safe anymore
Knife crime, guns and drug dealers have taken over
No child is safe, not anymore
The globe is warming and ice caps are melting
And sea levels are rising
Why let a poor baby live like this?
Oh how the world has changed!

**Courtnie Evelyn Hyland (12)**
Charles Burrell Humanities School, Thetford

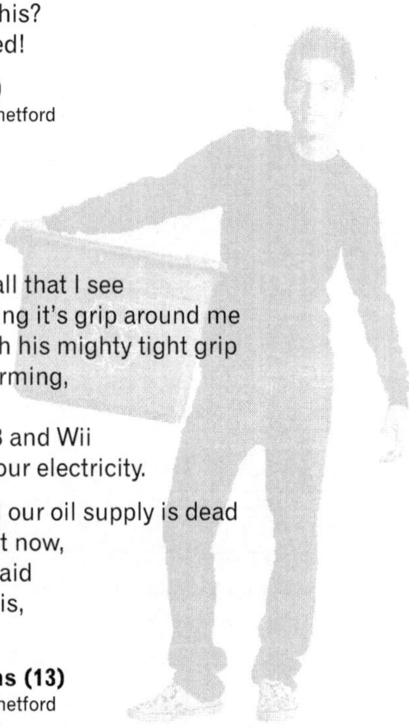

# The Green Mist

I look out of my window and all that I see
Is that big green mist tightening it's grip around me
He wraps round the Earth with his mighty tight grip
We all want to stop global warming,
But we just can't help it
Switch off your consoles, PS3 and Wii
Cos you see it's just wasting our electricity.

We're running out of coal and our oil supply is dead
So as you're sitting there right now,
You'd better listen to what's said
Because if we carry on like this,
We'll all definitely be dead!

**Aaron Scorer & Josh Cousins (13)**
Charles Burrell Humanities School, Thetford

# The World Is Falling Apart

The world is falling apart,
Why should we even care?
Think about everything and everyone on this planet,
That should care everyday.

The ice is melting all around the world
And we need you to help
Think about all the polar bears
That die everyday.

You should walk to school every day
To help save the world we live on
Tell your parents not to use the car too much
So they can save the planet too.

There are a lot more ways
To save our planet
So why don't you go and see
The world is falling apart
And that's why you should care.

**Danielle Moorhouse (12)**
Charles Burrell Humanities School, Thetford

# Alone!

Here I am on a cold paved floor,
With nothing but a blanket
I don't like sleeping here anymore
This is where I live
Mum kicked me out
I don't know what I did
I don't know what it's about.

I beg and I steal to get what I need
The police see if I am OK
I would like a wash
That's what I say -
Use a public toilet then
I sit and stare
I feel so bare.

**Lucy Claydon (13)**
Charles Burrell Humanities School, Thetford

# A Better Life!

Why do we always lose the precious ones!
Our mums, dads or beloved.
The ones that mean so much.
Afghanistan, Iraq and Oman.
We've lost so many.
Gunshots, bombs and late night attacks.
What a world we live in today.
Some people have survived
But it's sad to say not many
How would you feel if you had to tell your child
Their mummy or daddy wasn't coming home?
How must that feel?
Why are we doing this to the younger generation
Putting them through pain?
You shouldn't have to deal with this at such a young age.
So we will stand together
Let's try to stop these awful wars
Let's make people have a better life!

**Jessica Atkey (13)**
Charles Burrell Humanities School, Thetford

# The World

I give you life
You give me death
I give you forests
You give me fire.

I give you mountains
You give me cities
I give you sky
You give me fumes.

I give you friendship
You give me war
You give me false promises
I give you . . . *the end.*

**Callum Mastin-Myers (12)**
Charles Burrell Humanities School, Thetford

# The World Of Pollution

Even though the sky is grey,
Tomorrow will be another day,
Even though the pollution's still going
The grass in the park is still growing.

Even though the cars are still running
Doesn't mean the world's not stunning
Even though the air is black
Doesn't mean it can't come back.

Maybe if you stand up and say
The acid rain will go away
It's not too late to save the world
So tomorrow let's give it a whirl.

We're the only ones who can save this planet
It will take some time though
So don't forget we have to do it before it's too late
Or in a few years we'll meet our fate.

**Luke Jhon Betts (13)**
Charles Burrell Humanities School, Thetford

# Recycling Your Life

Recycle your life
Stop throwing rubbish
Recycle your life
Animals are dying
Recycle your life
Rainforests are losing life
Recycle your life
It is starting pollution
Recycle your life
And starting poverty
Recycle your life
Stop racism
Recycle your life
People are becoming homeless
Recycle your life.

**Megan Leigh-Anne Phipps (13)**
Charles Burrell Humanities School, Thetford

# Nuff Said

Don't use a car, begin cycling
Use the bins, start recycling
Stop being a litterbug
All this does is make you a thug
Save the Earth!

Don't release gas into the air
Leave stuff on standby, you don't care
Stop the wars
Choose a better cause
Save the Earth!

You don't care, why should I?
Let ice caps melt, polar bears die
All this extinction
Die with distinction
Nuff said!

**Daniel Harris (13)**
Charles Burrell Humanities School, Thetford

# Litter, Litter

Litter, litter everywhere
People drop it they don't care
Litter, litter on the street
Blowing freely about my feet.

Litter, litter we should care
Remember animals live down there
Tiny creatures at your feet
Live amongst litter from the street.

Litter, litter please find a bin
Do not drop it, it's a sin
Reuse, recycle, whatever the case
Let's make the world a better place.

**Chloe Standley (13)**
Charles Burrell Humanities School, Thetford

# Who Is This Little Fellow?

Keep going little fellow be brave and orbit the sun,
Please provide him with more energy
Recycled bottles would do the trick,
Help him by helping your community
Just save more water,
Please don't cut down the rainforests
Or he will have less oxygen to help him breathe,
No need to drop your litter 'bin it'
He could choke on it you know,
Engine fumes poison the air that we breathe in
But does this hurt our lungs?
Who is this little fellow?

**Alisha Switzer (13)**
Charles Burrell Humanities School, Thetford

# The Earth!

Why do we destroy our home?
Is it our greed?
Our anger?
Our selfishness?
Why do we kill the Earth's animals?
Is it our greed?
Our anger?
Our selfishness?
Why do we kill our friends and family?
Is it our greed?
Our lust for power?
Or territory?

**Ryan Holder (12)**
Charles Burrell Humanities School, Thetford

# Blood In My Eye

Eyes bleed from the heat of flames
I try to rise from the dirt on the ground
Mindless
Senseless
Same old fight with the same old outcome
A mother at home brokenhearted
Wondering how it all started
'Dear Mum, don't worry about me'
Last words I said to her before I left
'Why do we fight? Why do we fight?'

**Ashley Wood (13)**
Charles Burrell Humanities School, Thetford

# Saving The World - Haiku

Our world is dying
Right now we can all save it
Pollution stops here!

**Rhiannon Gray (12)**
Charles Burrell Humanities School, Thetford

# Green And Friendly

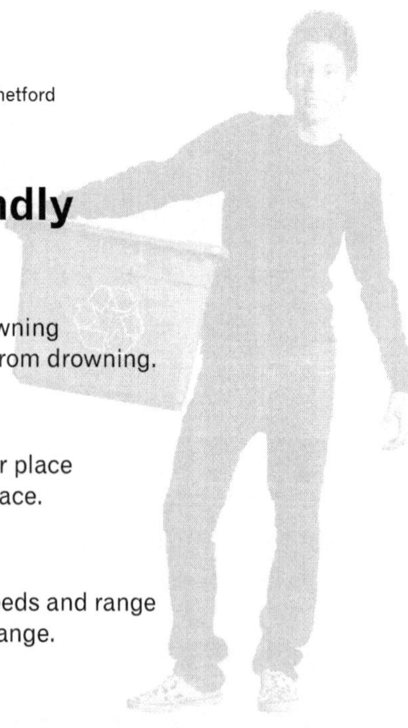

Don't be mean
Keep it green
Stop the polar bears from frowning
And stop the big wide world from drowning.

You are free
To plant a tree,
And help the world be a better place
And do your part for the eco-race.

The animals are crying
The plants are dying
This thing is killing all the breeds and range
It is all because of climate change.

**Rachel Appleby (11)**
Cromer High School, Cromer

# Windmills Or Landfills

Freshly cut grass
And picnic blankets
Sound of laughter
But five minutes after

The sky goes grey
But hey
Open your eyes
This may come as a surprise
Your Earth is fading away.

Back in the day
Your grandparents say
Waste not want not
But it seems we all forgot.

Gum's lost its taste
You know it's a waste
Throw it on the floor
Just like the time before.

Would you rather see
Beautiful scenery
Or a cut down tree?
So you decide!

*Windmills or landfills.*

**Connie Findlay, Leah Davies, Lauren Cook & Paige Nicholles (13)**
Cromer High School, Cromer

# Industry, Industry Everywhere

Up and down the motorways putting out gases,
Totally unaware that they're killing off the masses.
The vibrant colours red, blue and green,
It would all be better if they were seldom seen.

Industry, industry everywhere,
Chugging out poisons into the air.
Meeting demand and supplying the nation,
Better stop now or they will kill all creation.

Soaring through the air like regimented birds,
The noises overheard are too often heard.
The lines of kerosene litter the sky,
Cancel the flight or face a surprise.

Slicing the wood of the forests deep,
Totally inconsiderate of the animals asleep.
Constant logging to keep up the quota,
End it now or doom creeps closer.

The power is here, in the air,
Look all around you and wind is there.
The great turbines creak with strain,
They can make the Earth whole again.

Waves crashing against the shore,
Turning the turbines, like torrents of war.
The moon's power, drawn to Earth,
It's all in the water, riding on the surf.

The yellow and white beams going to waste,
Why not use them so we can replace,
All of the energy firing down,
It could be our saviour so use it now.

**Joe Phillips (15)**
Cromer High School, Cromer

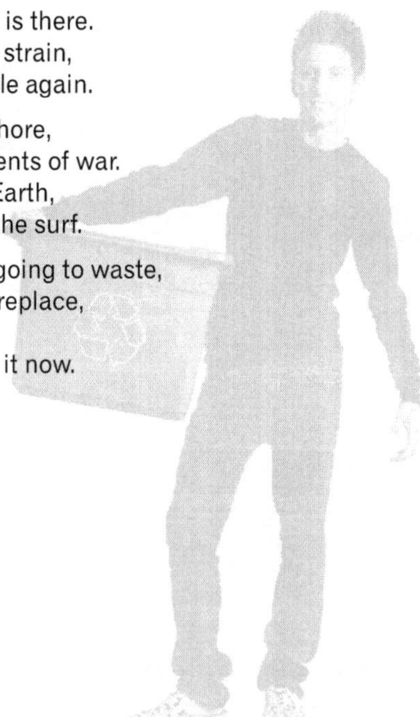

# Two Small Rocks Away From The Sun

Two small rocks away from the sun,
Lies a planet newly begun.
Clean blue oceans gently roll,
Beside lush green fields, hills and all.

See that tribe in the east of Sweden,
Slowly conquering this Garden of Eden;
Why, it's Man walking on two feet,
From far off lands long since deplete.

Slowly they spread, the ingenious group,
Forming towns and fogs of pea soup.
Over the Earth they tighten their grip,
Causing life and nature to slip.

Now here we are, facing global warming,
Having ignored natures good, great warning;
Our industrialisation and greedy fists
Have wreathed the Earth in poisonous mists.

Two small rocks away from the sun,
Lies a planet defeated and done,
Dark grey oceans cling like tar
Beside black cities near and far.

**Sean McNulty (15)**
Cromer High School, Cromer

# Help Recycle

The world needs your help,
So come on don't let the ice melt
And because of that you need to tighten your belt.
Reuse and recycle come on and help
Please save the penguins and polar bears,
So come on be someone that cares
And help me spread the word.
Reuse and recycle come on and help
We need to reduce our carbon footprint,
Because the world we know will cease to exist or worse,
Reuse and recycle come on and help.

**Sophie Nurse (13)**
Cromer High School, Cromer

# Beat Of My Heart

I'm homeless!
I sit on the street
My heart is keeping its beat.

No food, no clothes, no nothing!
I sit on the street
My heart keeping its beat.

I hate the cold!
I hate the people laughing!
My mouth goes watery
Whenever I see them eating,
I sit on the street
My heart keeping its beat.

My skin is dirty
My feet smell!
I haven't washed for ages!
I sit on the street
My heart keeping its beat.

No one loves me!
Because I'm *homeless!*

**Klaudia Golviowska (11)**
Cromer High School, Cromer

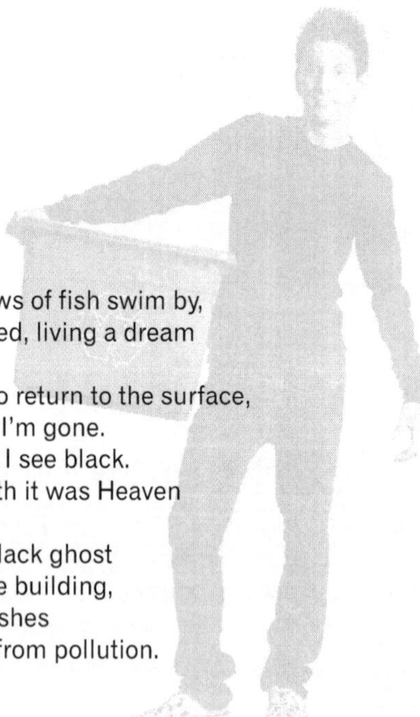

# World Explorer

I'm floating, watching rainbows of fish swim by,
Seaweed dances on the seabed, living a dream
Under the sea.
I'm running out of air I have to return to the surface,
One last glimpse around and I'm gone.
I look at the water around me I see black.
I don't understand, underneath it was Heaven
But now I can only see black.
I'm watching looking at the black ghost
Coming from the funnel of the building,
It glides into the sky and vanishes
The world needs to be saved from pollution.

**Yasmin Mantell (11)**
Cromer High School, Cromer

# Environment

Recycle, recycle
Paper, clothes and glass
It helps keep the world nice.

War, war
Bang, bang, death
Big war field.

Litter, litter
Messy stuff
Make the world clean.

Pollution, pollution
Walk to school
Cars make gases yuk!

Poverty, poverty
Poor, poor children
Give them a home.

Animals, animals
Help, help, help
Stop them from extinction.

**Gabrielle Richardson (11)**
Cromer High School, Cromer

# That Fur Coat!

Foxes, bears, rabbits and hares.
Dead to keep a person warm.
Why should they be harmed?

Why not wear fake, for animals' sake.
Why should they die, for people to buy?

When animals are no more
It will be a bore
No chasing, no running because of hunting
Do you want your pet, or rather regret.

Why not wear fake for animals' sake?
Why should they die, for people to buy?

**Chloe Lee (11)**
Cromer High School, Cromer

# The Lumbers

As a person approaches a tree,
And he gets chainsaws at the ready,
He saws into the tree steady, steady!
As his partner watches him saw,
And the machine is ready for the claw.
As he chops down the tree,
The claw gets so ready,
To pick the logs up, steady, steady!
As they pick the logs up, the lumber,
Their hearts start to pound
In case the cable comes loose
And plummets to the ground!
Someone up the top with a circular saw,
Cutting the cable!
As it plummets so fast
The lumbers dive and pray,
Maybe there last!
As the person at the top
Shouts so loud!
*Save Mother Nature!*

**Ross Johnstone (11)**
Cromer High School, Cromer

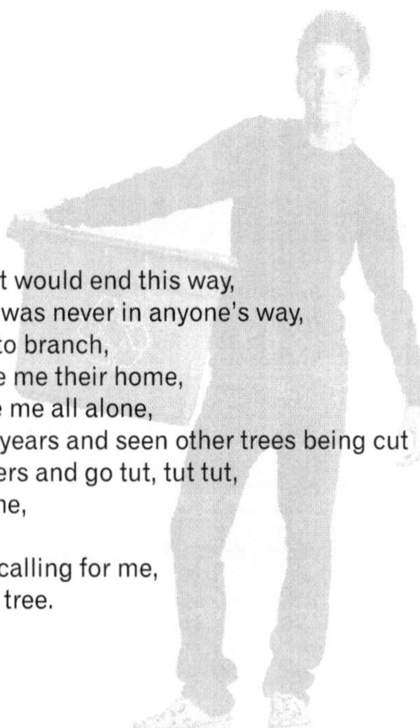

# The Old Tree

I have to say I never thought it would end this way,
I've been standing here and I was never in anyone's way,
Monkeys swing from branch to branch,
Birds nested on me and made me their home,
Then they would fly and leave me all alone,
I have been here for so many years and seen other trees being cut
I look down on the wood cutters and go tut, tut tut,
The saw went right through me,
I knew I was never left to be,
I heard the jungle death call, calling for me,
As I lay down as the dead old tree.

**Kirsty Clarke (11)**
Cromer High School, Cromer

# Recycle Now!

Recycling, recycling

Save the animals,
Icebergs melting and flushing us away,
Carbon footprint kicking us in the face,
Recycle, recycle
Before it's too late

Recycling, recycling

The world is heating up and its all our fault
What are our children going to see
When they grow up,
Recycle recycle,
We need your help.

Recycle, recycle

Look around litter everywhere
Look around, cars clashing
Look around, species disappearing
Look around, global warming.

**Laura Cross Fulcher (13)**
Cromer High School, Cromer

# Save The Rainforest!

Poppies are red, blueberries are blue,
Help save the rainforest
That's the good in you!
The monkeys are dying
The people are crying.
I like the rainforests
So that's why I'm trying.
Save the trees, save them please
Because I am begging on my knees!
Think of the world, yes save it please,
The animals need help
And when they are being killed,
They let out a *yelp!*

**John Lee (11)**
Cromer High School, Cromer

# Why?

In this land of sin and fallen angels,
Where the prophecies and proclamations
Of tyrannical leaders hold as much depth and meaning
As a shallow pool of nothingness,
A single thought inhabits the almost hive-mentality
Of the droves of common people.
Blissfully unaware of the destruction
Of everything that holds wonder,
Delight and awe in this world,
The thought is: 'more, I must have more material possessions'
The planet is raped and pillaged
As we fill our pockets with worthless riches,
Things like gold, silver and priceless jewels,
These mean nothing after the truly precious gift
Of life passes into the afterlife,
As people fight and kill
Over religion and social standing,
I watch in disbelief and ask myself: 'why?'

**Joseph John Stanley Guthrie (15)**
Cromer High School, Cromer

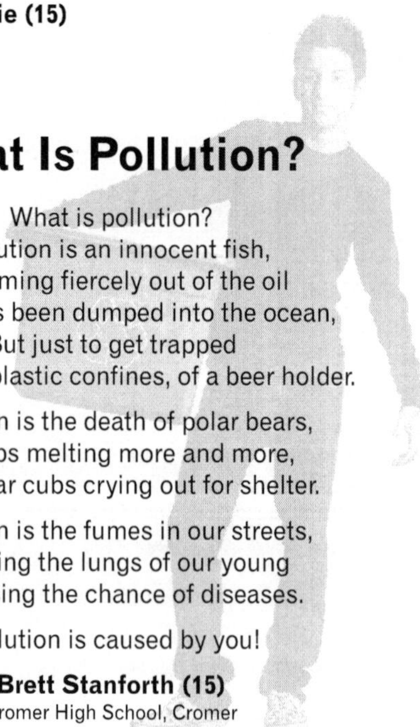

# What Is Pollution?

What is pollution?
Pollution is an innocent fish,
Swimming fiercely out of the oil
Which has been dumped into the ocean,
But just to get trapped
Within the plastic confines, of a beer holder.

Pollution is the death of polar bears,
Ice caps melting more and more,
Polar bear cubs crying out for shelter.

Pollution is the fumes in our streets,
Infecting the lungs of our young
Increasing the chance of diseases.

Pollution is caused by you!

**Brett Stanforth (15)**
Cromer High School, Cromer

# Tiger

In a two by two cage
Solid, metal, hard.
I'm skinny all bones
It's not right.

Nothing to eat
No water around
Nothing but bones that's me.

People poking
Staring and joking
I hate it so I growl.

I'm wild free
Running free
If only it could be

I'm scared, I'm stuck
Now take me death and
End the pain *please.*

**Hannah Carter (11)**
Cromer High School, Cromer

# Being Green Animal Poem

A nimal, animal,
N ow endangered,
I t needs to stop now,
M en hunting,
A nimal, animals,
L ove animals.

H elp the animals,
U se your knowledge,
N ow is the time,
T oday is the day,
I n danger,
N eeds help now,
G o help them *now!*

It's up to you to save animals!

**Jemma Flaxman (11)**
Cromer High School, Cromer

# How Full Is Your Recycling Bin?

How full is your recycling bin?
From my point of view, it should be up to the rim!
There's loads of things that we use everyday
That can go in the bin, there's more than I can say!

How full is your recycling bin?
There's toilet paper tubes, and tin,
Things that we use a lot, anything recyclable that you've got!

How full is your recycling bin?
Wheel it out on the day, the bin man comes,
He puts it in his lorry, he isn't in a hurry,
So run after him with bits of card and paper!

How full is your recycling bin?
He takes it to a factory and it is squashed
And made into something else you see,
And if you do this, you'll be doing your part,
And you can put a tick on your big green chart!

**Alice Dawson (11)**
Cromer High School, Cromer

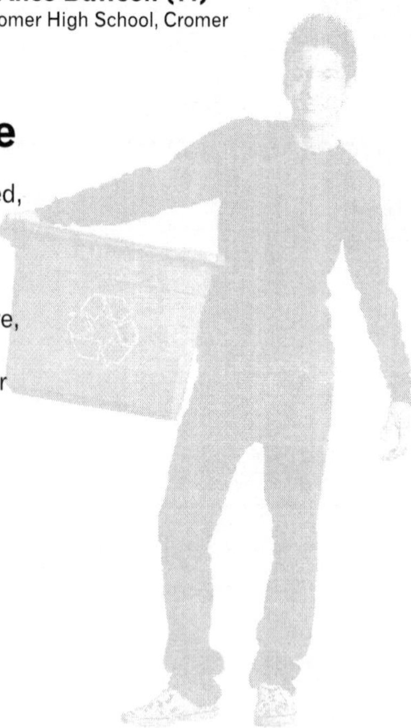

# Use Your Bicycle

Environment is being destroyed,
So use your bicycle,
Pollution is getting Stronger,
So use your bicycle,
Don't pollute the Earth no more,
So use your bicycle,
If you don't stop wasting paper
The Earth will soon die,
So use your bicycle,
Use,
Your,
Bicycle,
It's as easy as A, B, C
Basically!

**Georgina Burrows (11)**
Cromer High School, Cromer

## Do Something Soon!

If we don't do something soon the world will end,
The ice and the ozone is what we need to mend,
Global warming is spreading fast,
If we don't do something soon this world will never last.

Do you recycle?
I hope you do,
Don't hide from the fact there's things you do wrong too,
Card, paper and tin,
Are all things that can go in the recycling bin.

Endangered animals are everywhere,
Try to help if you really care,
For those animals don't you feel for,
Never being able to hear the lions' roar,
The poor little things are scared and alone,
So do something soon
And we'll not hear them moan.

**Louisa Hadley (11)**
Cromer High School, Cromer

## Our Home

The world,
The world is full of cars,
The cars pollute the world,
The world,
The world is being destroyed.

The Earth,
The Earth is protected by the ozone,
The ozone is destroyed by pollution,
The Earth,
The Earth is being destroyed.

Our planet,
Our planet is dying,
Our planet is our home,
Our home
*We* are destroying our home.

**Michael Gray (11)**
Cromer High School, Cromer

# Who Is To Blame?

The rainforest is in danger,
Danger of you,
If people don't stop cutting down trees
They will be gone, gone forever,
The animals are starting to disappear,
Because of the invisible trees,
It will be gone forever,
No food,
No drink,
No family,
It will be gone forever
How would you feel?
You would die in sadness,
So just think
The beauty of the rainforest
Is in your hands.

**Gemma Harris (11)**
Cromer High School, Cromer

# The Rainforest

People chopping the trees down
This sort of thing makes people frown
All the species getting pushed out
They will be extinct soon without a doubt.

All the trees are fighting for life
Just so the farmer can feed his wife
As his cattle slowly graze
Some trees get destroyed in the blaze.

So the choice is yours
Don't think I'm a bore
So do your bit
And take a trip
And save the rainforest.

**Rosie Marwick (15)**
Cromer High School, Cromer

# Homeless!

Being homeless is not great
It is lonely, sad and cold
I don't eat or drink
I could die at any moment in time
Maybe my mother and father will be back for me
I want to cry but am being brave
People think that being homeless is fun
But they are wrong it is horrible
So please treat us with respect
Because we are all the same
But us homeless people are only
Different because we have
*No home!*

**Abygail Betts (11)**
Cromer High School, Cromer

# The Suffering World

He coughed
Then stumbled around the sun once more
He squinted through the fog,
To see the moon waving at him
As he does another round
As the years go past it gets worse
Maybe I need glasses,
*I can't see a thing* he thought
Where does the fog come from
Where does it come from?

**Odette Hilder (15)**
Cromer High School, Cromer

# Mean Or Green

Are you being green or are you being mean?
Are you helping out?
Do you go and shout?
Do you let the world know?
Do you help the world show?
It needs help
Let it out of the economical strife
It isn't right it should be helped
You should be told before you grow old
Help and help now.

**Sophie Abel (11)**
Cromer High School, Cromer

# The Monster

The monster's growing
Dropping litter on the ground
And leaving on lights.

It's engulfing the Earth
With its intoxicating fumes
Murdering all life.

Numinous Earth's gone
Caused by the monster that is us
Don't let this be.

**Nicola Gray (15)**
Cromer High School, Cromer

## I'm Green Are You?

I'm green are you?
If you aren't how come?
What did you do?
Did you blow something up
Or use too many fossil fuels?
Did you use a petrol car?
Buy a G-Whizz!
Be environmentally friendly
And the world will be nicer!

**Creed Finnegan (12)**
Cromer High School, Cromer

## Pollution

P ollution kills,
O ver the world,
L iving a life,
L onely and shy,
U nder the sun,
T ill noon rises,
I diots are stupid,
O ver the world,
N ever be one yourself.

**Kelsy Gudgeon (11)**
Cromer High School, Cromer

## Litter, Litter, Litter

The litter here is disgusting
It is just a dusting
As we tip we flip
With all that dirty rubbish
Laziness or just plain dumb
As we tip we are destroying our world
Our world . . .
*Our world . . .*

**Elliot Verrier (11)**
Cromer High School, Cromer

# Racism Against The World

Think before you speak
We're all the same inside
Don't leap and mock people's
Different *shades*
Because we're all
The same
Inside!

**Sarah Nash (12)**
Cromer High School, Cromer

# Dying

Our planet is dying,
The people are crying,
So why aren't you trying to save it?
It's getting hotter
Too hot for an otter
So now we won't survive.

**Henry Cross-Fultcher (12)**
Cromer High School, Cromer

# Polar Bears Stranded On A Tiny Ice Cube

Polar bears stranded on a tiny ice cube,
Crumbling beneath their feet,
They cling to the ice cubes
As the world melts beneath
As ice cream melts in the sun
In the summer.

**Abigail Clipsom (15)**
Cromer High School, Cromer

# Green

Green is wicked,
Green is cool,
Green will save the world,
Green don't act like a fool,
So will you help green?
Save the planet today?

**Robert Cox (12)**
Cromer High School, Cromer

# What Will Happen?

What will happen when the ozone's gone?
What will happen when the last polar bear dies?
What will happen when the last fish is caught?
What will happen when the sea overcomes us?
*Where are we?*

**Tom Brodie (12)**
Cromer High School, Cromer

# The World I Call My Own

The grass is green,
The sky is blue,
Soon to be demolished . . .

We should do
What they did for us,
Keep the world polished . . .

The world is precious,
Use it that way,
So think about this every day . . .

What kind of world is this,
This world I call my own?
I will have to pay . . .

But so will you.

**Jasmine Coventry (14)**
Diss High School, Diss

# I Love It When You Fly . . .

I love it when you fly . . .
Gliding across that clear, unpolluted water,
Propelled by that clean wind.
Out of control; where is the wind?
It plays with you like a cat plays with a spider.
It pounces when you least expect.
You use it, not exploit it, use it . . .
The wind helps you.

I love it when you fly . . .
Cutting through the water like a knife
Slicing through your obstacles.
You, silently baiting, hooking, taking the wind.
You dance smoothly to your destination,
Never luffing, see the birds, love where you are.
You walk on with the water where others,
Stutter, lurch, noisily, smelly fumes clinging to the air,
Startling nests, upsetting everyone and everything, everywhere.

I love it when you fly . . .
The music of the water is like the twinkling of the stars at night,
Magical, making you follow like a Will-o'-the-wisp's secretive lanterns,
Or a writer drawing you into their bound labour of love.

I love it when you fly . . .
Down blue paths no one can walk, an orchestra of ripples
Lap at your hull of joy,
Playing the most quiet, most intricate, most natural music
No one could write, no one can describe it,
No one cannot enjoy it,
No one human cannot love it.

I love it when you fly . . .
Sail where you want to sail, see what you want to see,
Hear what you want to hear.
Steering a wooden boat is as nature-friendly as possible.

I love it when you fly . . .
Alter to the wind, it won't alter to you.
A figure of eight and a half hitch will help you on your way.
You're ever trimmed, primed like an assassin's gun
Ready for any change.
Never go the shortest route, but ask the wind where to go.
Tack with the tension of the sails,
Heeling over to the wind's bidding.

I love it when you fly . . .
It's the best way to travel . . .
Weaving with the wind . . .
Better than motors . . .
Better than using nature . . .
Enjoy nature.

**Robin Breeze (13)**
Diss High School, Diss

# Once Upon A Time . . .

Once upon a time,
When the world was created,
The birds flew freely
And the atmosphere was whole.

Dolphins swam gracefully
And horses ran peacefully.
There was no rubbish floating in the sea,
Or cars polluting the sweet air.

Life was calm, no worries at all,
There was no such thing as factories
Or greenhouse gases, or chemical pollution.
Life was healthy and pure.

Polar bears lived happily
And the rainforest was carefree.
The beautiful countryside had not been destroyed
And animals had not been harmed.

That was the past and this is the present.
Life has changed, mankind has changed.
We need to stop it now,
Before it gets out of control.

So turn off your lights,
And turn down your heating.
Turn off your electrical items
And maybe our grandchildren
Will see a polar bear.

**Hannah Lane (13)**
Diss High School, Diss

# *Beep, Beep,* The Sound Of The Planet Killer

We see people driving around in their metal cages,
We don't question that they do.
Millions of them exist,
Millions of the terrible killing beasts.

Shiny metal beasts of destruction
That spit out poisonous gases
That we pay so much for
But are just waiting to slit our throats.

We feed them
Clean them
And in return
They destroy our environment.

But there is a way.
I have seen the future

A future in which we need not
Burn dead creatures to get around
A future where the world is safe
And the future is bright

It does not need any real thought
In fact it takes none at all
We just need a change of attitude

If we walk it does no real harm,
If we bike we can go far
If we travel by bus it's less damage
If we travel by train we can go long distances

So in this world of new technology,
Is it not barbaric to dig up the remains
Of long dead plants, trees and animals and burn them?

We see new forms of power being born
Solar, tidal, wind and many more
So is not burning stuff a little old-fashioned?

**James Baxter (13)**
Diss High School, Diss

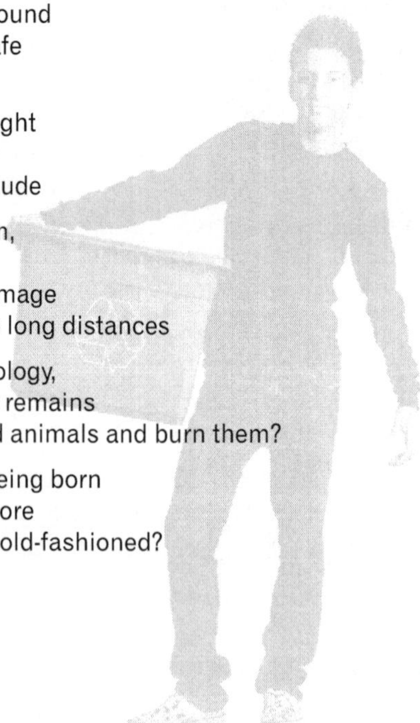

# Do You Really Need All Those Plastic Bags?

I went shopping the other day,
Just to Tesco with my mum.
And as she started loading the food,
I said to her, 'Mum, do you *really* need all those plastic bags?'

100 years they take to rot,
100 years to decompose.
100 years, that's a long time,
*You* might not even live that long; imagine that.

But what, I hear you ask . . .
But what can *I* do to help?
Well all it is, is the three Rs,
Reduce, reuse and recycle.

Or you could buy a 'bag for life',
Everyone sells them,
In cool sizes and colours,
Perfect for anyone and everyone!

So next time you go to the shop
And buy a bunch of goodies,
Just ask yourself . . .
Do I *really* need a plastic bag?

**Madison Turner (13)**
Diss High School, Diss

# Litter

I lie on the floor every day,
I get stood on every day,
I get friends more and more,
It's getting a little crowded now . . .
No one thinks to pick me up,
Once in a while my friends get picked up
But they soon come back again.
Still getting trodden on,
Still here . . .

**Shannon Edwards (11)**
Diss High School, Diss

# Some Scars Never Heal

Is it right to take a child away from its parent?

She nestled her head in her teddy
Her mother was about to be jailed

Is it fair to blame the crime on the child?
Because it's the child who suffers without its parent

And as you were about to leave
A little hand cautiously tugs at your uniform

A striking pair of big, brown eyes stare up at you
With red lips quivering

This restrained, tiny voice made a request

'Mister, please don't take my mummy away'
Your heart falls from your chest

You agonise with this innocent child
Your heart is completely shattered

Your mind fills with thoughts of
What if this was my baby
Pleading with a stranger to spare her mummy

Your eyes blurred with tears
Although you knew what you would not say

Only the understanding for the little one forced
A love for this baby
Perhaps one which you had reserved for your own children

You wanted her to know the joy of a real family
This wonderful child loved in every way
The world she lives in is full of pain
A little face with big tears

Some scars never heal.

**Emily Pilsbury-Gaunt (13)**
Diss High School, Diss

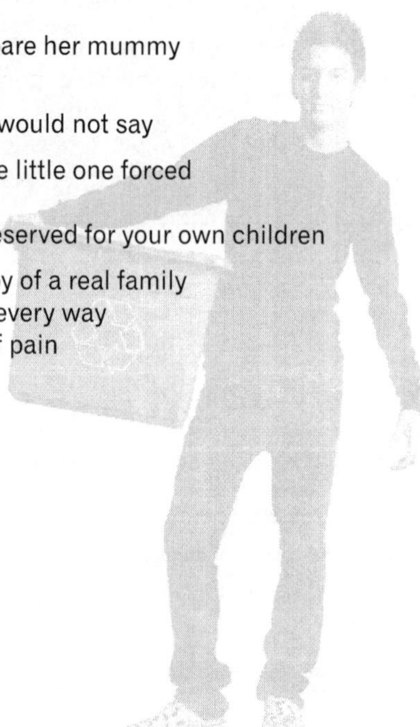

# The Big Issue

We're destroying the Earth as we know it.
Day by day it's slowly changing.
Landfills growing, Earth is slowing,
Waiting to die, forever.

This is because
Species of animals are disappearing,
Never to be seen again.
They are all dying in pain,
So very, very quickly.

This is because of destroying rainforests,
Loggers logging miles a minute,
Killing the world's lungs,
Never to breathe again.

This is because of resources going away
By us sat on our chairs eating, making ourselves fat,
Making our greenhouse gases,
Popping off, using cars to pop down the road,
Not saving electricity.

This is melting the ice caps,
Killing off polar bears,
Slowly drowning the world.

So now's the time to act,
Get off your chair, buy a bike,
Turn the TV off
And reduce, reuse, recycle.
Save the trees,
*Save the world!*

**Connor Baines (13)**
Diss High School, Diss

# Save The World!

When the world began, everything was right
The trees were green, the seas were blue
Night was dark and day was light

But now look what has happened
The mess we've gotten into
The harm we've done, the right and wrong
And the political issues

It's all because of us; we've done this to ourselves
We've got to change, we've got to learn
So here starts our challenge to save the world

We've got to recycle, we've got to reuse
Time's ticking away
The world's on a short fuse!

So turn to thirty and stop using cars
Stop the polluting!
We can't move to Mars!

I've changed and you can too
We've got to take action!
Now it's up to you!

*Save the world!*

**Katherine Phillips (13)**
Diss High School, Diss

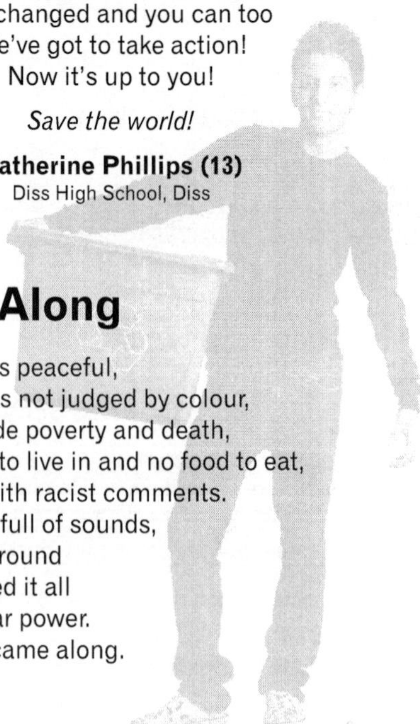

# Until We Came Along

A long time ago the world was peaceful,
Everyone had a home and was not judged by colour,
Until we came along and made poverty and death,
With people having no home to live in and no food to eat,
With bullying and sadness, with racist comments.
This world was beautiful and full of sounds,
Trees so big with animals surround
Until we came along and killed it all
With our pollution and nuclear power.
The world was nice until we came along.

**Mary Dunning (14)**
Diss High School, Diss

# No Ice

White speck surrounded in endless blue
Looking for land where once was
Travelling for days and days
In the most freezing water
That you could only dream of
Desperately, frantically looking for a place to rest
Desperately, frantically looking for a bit of meat
Once the land was found
Its body was so exhausted, so drained
It could not barely get on to its feet
It lay there hopelessly
Unknowing whether it would survive
Luckily it did
In ten years' time
When its child goes looking for food
On the same route
It might not live to see land
That its father survived with
So next time
When you turn your heating up just that one degree
When you take an unnecessary car journey
Think of that polar bear with no ice.

**Surjay Rughani (13)**
Diss High School, Diss

# Melting Away

At the Arctic where it's icy and cold,
There are massive icebergs, they're great and bold.
The average temperature is -20,
Too hot for polar bears, soon it will be empty.
Unless we turn to 30, and stop driving cars,
Get energy-saving bulbs, because we can't just move to Mars.
We've got to try and save the Earth,
To show the planet what she is worth.
So stop leaving the TV on standby all day
To stop the ice from melting away.

**Naomi Loome (14)**
Diss High School, Diss

# Save Our Planet!

Icebergs are melting,
Polar bears are dying,
The sea level is rising,

What can you do?

The world was once perfect,
With no pollution at all.
Save the animals,
Before the ice gets too small.

What can you do?

Countries will have gone by the next generation,
We need to stop this disaster from happening!

What can you do?

Trees are disappearing,
People are getting greedy,
The rich have lots of money,
But what about the needy?

What can you do?

Save our planet and the animals!

**Katherine Knights (13)**
Diss High School, Diss

# The Enemy

The skies were blue, an ocean blue.
The trees were green, an emerald green.
The air was clean, what have they done?
Now the fires of the forest are burning, burning bright,
The animals are helpless, hunted and afraid,
The people who are destroying, dangerous and deadly,
They are selfish, careless and the enemy.
The trees are chopped and taken from their home,
The animals are fading and their homes burn away,
The people are destroying, dangerous and deadly,
They are selfish, careless and the enemy.

**Emma Youngs (13)**
Diss High School, Diss

# Revolution

Litter and pollution
We need a revolution.

Rubbish is getting out of hand
We need to clean up all our land.

More litter bins
To collect the empty tins.

We're hurting ourselves, wrecking our own lives
Ignoring people's silent cries and thrives.

Litter and pollution
We need a revolution.

We could save this world today,
Something we've done and we should pay,
By walking to work a street away,
Or using one of those bags for life or so they say.

Give our children a better life,
Not one we've ruined and then died.

Litter and pollution
We need a revolution.

**Jade Fraser (13)**
Diss High School, Diss

# Where Have All The Animals Gone?

The loneliness of a panda
Means his family has gone.

The sadness of a baby chimp
Means his mother has gone.

A starving polar bear
Means the energy to hunt has gone.

The last of your kind
Means the rest have gone.

The danger of animals going extinct
Doesn't have to mean the hope is gone.

**Eleanor Missen (13)**
Diss High School, Diss

# What's The Point?

What's the point
In dropping litter?
What's the point
In making people starve?
What's the point
In killing animals?
What's the point
In cutting down trees?
What's the point
In melting ice caps?
What's the point
In murdering another?
What's the point
In being racist?
What's the point
In using cars?
So tell me,
What's the point?

**Martin Stubbs (13)**
Diss High School, Diss

# All Gone Away

We used to see them every day,
Soon they'll all be gone away.

Elephant tusk, so pure and white,
Hacked off, stolen in the night.

Tiger, graceful, proud and true,
Killed for fur for me and you.

Apes, monkeys, chimps and baboons,
Illegal bush meat, taken too soon.

Giant turtles hide in their shells,
Trophy hunters take them as well.

We used to see them every day,
Now they're all gone, away.

**Lauren Brown (13)**
Diss High School, Diss

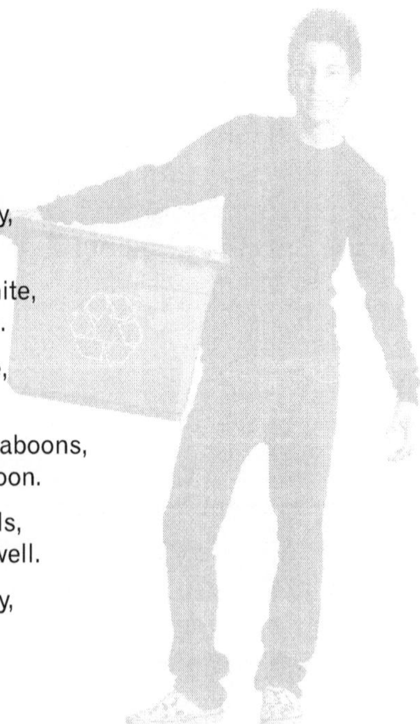

## The Streets

I walk the street,
Day in, day out
People point and laugh
Call me names
'Oi, stinky!' they shout
They don't understand
It's the same every day
Walk around, rest,
Then move
At night I fear for my life
Will I be here tomorrow?
Sometimes I hope I'm not
I long to find a home
Somewhere to keep me safe
Feed me, clean me
And keep me warm
I can dream and hope
I'll find it soon.

**Sophie Brooks (14)**
Diss High School, Diss

## Wish

*If I had only one wish*
*It would not be for a car*
*Not even that new album out*
*Or a brand new high-tech park*

If I had only one wish
It wouldn't be for world peace
Or more posters on my bedroom door
That game that came out yesterday
But if I only had one wish

I'd wish for no more pollution
No more cars with petrol
And no more chopping down trees
This is what I would wish.

**Josh Moore (13)**
Diss High School, Diss

# Poverty Is Bad!

Poverty is bad
It makes me mad
People homeless
And always sad

Poverty is everywhere
If only we gave a care
In lots of countries
Here and there

Poverty is around the world
You wouldn't like to live in mould
Or live in damp
And live in cold.

Poverty is bad
It makes me mad
People homeless
And always sad.

**Jemma Lee (13)**
Diss High School, Diss

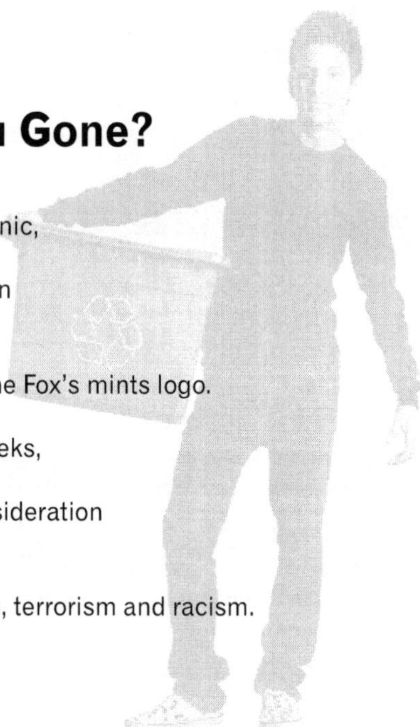

# Where Have You Gone?

Where have you gone?
The iceberg that sunk the Titanic,
Where have you gone,
The tree that gives food to Man
And animals alike,
Where have you gone?
The polar bear that inspired the Fox's mints logo.
Where have you gone?
The family that starved for weeks,
Where have you gone?
Justice, stewardship and consideration
Where have you gone?
I can tell you they are lost
In a world of poverty, pollution, terrorism and racism.
*Now, where are you*?

**Sam Denham Cain (14)**
Diss High School, Diss

# The Green

The green everywhere,
So beautiful you would stare.
Now we have buildings, roads,
All the mess,
All of it covering the green.

But the technology,
All the things we can do,
What's important, the world or you?
Polluting the world can be bad,
But if people use less,
Will people be sad?

But overall, we should think,
Everything happening in one blink.
Help by using less and less,
And maybe one day,
We won't have all this mess.

**April Disney (13)**
Diss High School, Diss

# Bang!

I'm running through the forest
Running for my life.
I see my comrades falling down
I wonder if I'll ever make it.
I see my life flash before me
I once dreamed of having a family
It's all gone now
I see my brother
It's not possible, he's dead
Because of the war
I'm so young,
What a waste of time
Before I know it
*Bang!*
Why do we have to fight.

**Steffan Wilby (11)**
Diss High School, Diss

# A Darker World

The world is becoming darker.

Carbon emissions and pollution are adding to the greenhouse effects
And the greenhouse effect is adding to climate change
And therefore the world is becoming darker.

People are burning fossil fuels, which adds carbon dioxide to the atmosphere.
The Arctic is melting and polar bears are dying.
The world is becoming darker.

The seasons are changing, winter is now summer and summer is now winter.
Crime rates are higher and jail populations are increasing.
All because the world is becoming darker.

**Liam Rackham (13)**
Diss High School, Diss

# The Rainforest

The planet,
Our home,
Our life,
Yet we strip her bare,
You really think this is fair.

Once a wonderful place,
Full of life,
Now a place of shadows,
Death and corruption.

Our lives of luxury only at the cost
Of our real luxury,
Our planet.

**Michael Greenard (14)**
Diss High School, Diss

# I Wish

I wish one day Man will walk on Mars
And look back at Earth,
Seeing a shiny emerald enveloped in dark.
I wish polar bars wouldn't have to battle an endless sea
In desperate pursuit of disappearing ice.
I wish armies in their millions would see a foe
As they saw themselves - just as innocent.
I wish hot, humid rainforests would still be blooming
In years or centuries to come.
I wish a huge tsunami crashed in Cuba
But the rest of the world helped in an instant.
If only 'I wish' was 'it is'.

**Angus Barnett (13)**
Diss High School, Diss

# I Am A Young Polar Bear

You are melting the ice,
I have no food.
You are melting my ice,
I can't catch food.
There are only a few of me,
Not many cubs,
Sometimes mothers can't catch food,
And we all have to starve.
It is getting a lot warmer out here,
You are killing all my friends.
Just think, save the polar bear
And be my best friend.

**Sharna Eldred (11)**
Diss High School, Diss

# The Street

Nowhere to go,
Always walk, hot and cold,
People look and stare,
They say, 'Ugh! Look at him,
He's a mess.'
They don't understand.
I don't have a home,
I have no money,
I have nothing,
Nowhere to sleep,
It gets scary sometimes
At night on the street.

**Ashley Emms (12)**
Diss High School, Diss

# Green Machine Poem

We want to save the planet,
So recycling's what we'll do,
All our plastic cartons,
Bottles and cans too.

Small contributions such as recycling,
Stop global warming,
Global warming is killing the planet,
Anything small will help, we must not panic!

Before you go to bed at night,
Remember to turn off the lights,
Save the icebergs and the polar bears.

**Mitchell Vale (13)**
Diss High School, Diss

# Out On The Ice

Out on the ice what can I see?
I see the beautiful, blue ocean
Spread out before me,
Glistening in the fading sunlight.

Out on the ice what can I see?
I see the peaceful polar bears,
Curled up on the small, colourless iceberg,
Exhaunsted, stranded, frightened.

Out on the ice what can I see?
I see . . . well, nothing,
Just the dark, lifeless ocean, spread out before me.

**James Briddon (13)**
Diss High School, Diss

# The Rainforest

A beautiful land that spreads for miles,
Tropical flowers,
High green trees,
Songs and sounds of the precious creatures,
But that's yesterday.

A land that shrinks day by day,
Burning greens,
Chainsaws ringing,
Animals screaming,
Disappearing beauty,
That's today!

**Nicola Elliston (14)**
Diss High School, Diss

# The Street Life

I wander the streets,
Wondering what's going to happen next,
Where to sleep, whether I will live?
People look at me and laugh
And call me names,
They just don't know what it's like
To live on streets.
Step by step I worry
If I will ever live in a home
Where people will love me and care for me.
Still dreaming now.

**Louise Owen (11)**
Diss High School, Diss

# Pollution

This is a poem about pollution
And hoping one day there will be a solution.
It makes us sneeze, it makes us cough,
It makes a lot of people rough.
We try to walk and not use the car,
But sometimes it seems it's just too far.
The factories' chimneys give out smoke,
That's enough to make us choke.
The country air is what we need,
Clean up pollution - that's what we plead.

**Travis Andrew Quelch (14)**
Diss High School, Diss

## We Need To Help These People

We need to help these people,
It really makes me sad,
To see how very bad
These poor, poor people are
In these places like Africa.
We need to help these people
Out there all alone,
Thirsty, hungry,
Dirty, diseased,
Help these people please, please, please.

**Clare Lanchester (13)**
Diss High School, Diss

## War

What is war?
War is here to hurt us, war is here to stay.
Wherever I go, there's war, war, war.
You can see it, you can hear it,
But you can't stop it.
War is here to stay unless we make it go away.
Go on war, run away.
War was here to hurt us,
But now war has gone away.

**Amy Harding (13)**
Diss High School, Diss

## Death

*Bang! Bang!* Dead on the floor,
The blood is leaking more and more,
Shot in the skull,
Into the brain,
Life is going like a slowing train.
War . . .

**Jethro Mason (11)**
Diss High School, Diss

# War Cries

I walked one day past a war memorial
And I looked up high,
I remembered the British soldiers who did die.
I remembered my grandad with pride
And I saw the pain beneath his eyes.

I don't get war, they die
And they feel the emotion of their families,
But their families hear the cry of pain.

**Kyle Cook-Barnes (11)**
Diss High School, Diss

# $CO_2$

$CO_2$, $CO_2$
All they want is $CO_2$
Driving cars
Going on planes
Why do they like $CO_2$?
All it does
Is destroy our Earth
So let's cut down on $CO_2$.

**Cem Cilfaoglu (14)**
Diss High School, Diss

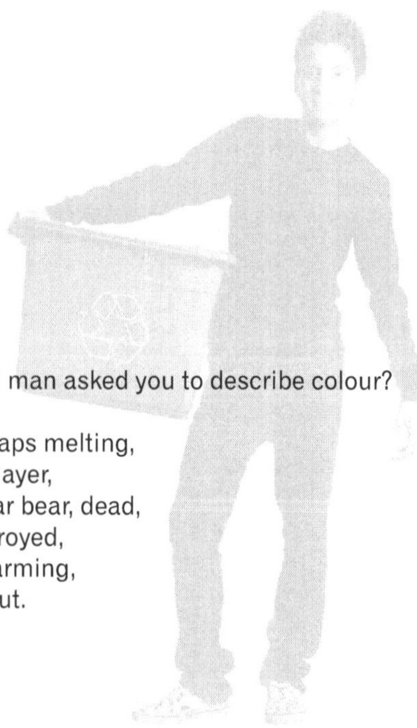

# Blindness

What would you say if a blind man asked you to describe colour?
Would you say . . .
Blue is the colour of the ice caps melting,
Blue is the hole in the ozone layer,
White is the once mighty polar bear, dead,
Green is the Earth being destroyed,
Red is the colour of global warming,
Black is the last light going out.

**Anthony Punt (13)**
Diss High School, Diss

# Recycling Is Us

Rubbish is smelly, rubbish is bad
If you drop it, you must be mad
Everywhere you see it, every time it's there
Don't drop it, don't you dare
Don't drop rubbish, you'll pollute our land
Don't drop rubbish, just keep it in your hand
That's the poem, we'll leave it to you
Just make sure you know what to do.

**James Pipe & Hayden Leeder (13)**
Diss High School, Diss

# Imagine

Imagine a world with no poverty or suffering,
A world where every living person has a decent way of life.
Imagine a world where there is enough food to satisfy everyone.
Imagine a world without slavery or abuse,
A world where every man and woman is equal,
Nothing to restrict people from their rights and fairly earned wages.
Can you imagine a world like this?
I can.

**Charlie Pask (13)**
Diss High School, Diss

# Racism

People teasing you for the colour of your skin,
People punching you for where you used to live.
Black people scared to go out at night,
They're scared they're going to get into a fight.
This is what's happening everywhere,
Racism shouldn't be a game,
Racists have to realise that everyone's the same.

**Emilie Holdsworth (14)**
Diss High School, Diss

# Why Drop Me?

Why do children drop me?
Just leave me here to rot.
Can't they drop me in a bin
To stop me killing nature?
Why drop me?
I smell very funny
When I start to rot.

**Sarah Litchfield (12)**
Diss High School, Diss

# Poverty Doesn't Have To Happen

If everyone were equal, there would be no poverty.
If everyone were equal there would be no war,
There would be sharing and friendship throughout the world.
Poverty doesn't have to happen,
We can stop it if we help other countries with their money
And make everyone equal,
Poverty doesn't have to happen.

**Harriet Carter (13)**
Diss High School, Diss

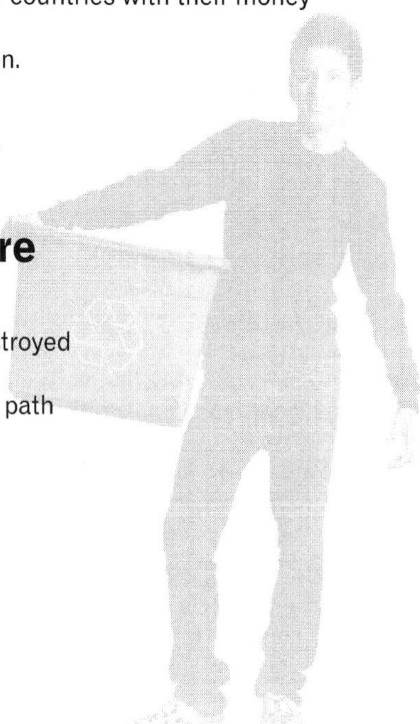

# Hanging In There

I hang in the trees
Watching our home being destroyed
Metal machines are coming
Destroying everything in their path
We fight for our lives
What will happen?

**Sean Thompson (11)**
Diss High School, Diss

# Litter

Litter, litter, litter, it's everywhere!
Why do people drop litter?
Why can't people recycle like some others do?
Just take some time to recycle,
Rather than dropping litter about.
Put it in a bin or keep it in your pocket.

**Neethu Sebastian (13)**
Diss High School, Diss

# Litter

L itter everywhere, where should it go?
I wish it was sorted out
T issues here, tissues there
T ake the litter away, far away
E nvironment needs sorting out
R ubbish, I hate it.

**Alice Bateson (11)**
Diss High School, Diss

# War - Haiku

Planes fly overhead
Screaming children, shooting guns
*Boom! Bang!* People dead.

**Jack Foster (13)**
Diss High School, Diss

# Earth's Coming To An End

The stars fall from the heavens
Earth is becoming Hell
Animals dying
Animals suffering
And we're comfy
Earth is coming to an end
But safety's round the bend
Now the war came
And we're the ones to blame
The bang of the gun
The scream of someone's son
Stop the killing
Change the law
Close the door of war.

**Joshua Nathan Hart (11)**
Elm Tree Middle School, Lowestoft

# Logging, Melting, Pollution Kills

Animals are dying
for the conditions
are no longer bearable
Monkeys are trying
for jungles are disappearing
for the machines
are cutting them down.
For machines
are melting the ice caps.
So the penguins
are dying due
to less land
pollution kills.

**Samuel King (11)**
Elm Tree Middle School, Lowestoft

# I Stay Stop!

I say *stop*
Putting rubbish in the sea
I say *stop*
Ruining nature for you and me

I say *stop*
Killing the animals, they haven't done wrong
I say *stop*
Sitting there singing along

I say *stop*
Costing yourself a life
I say *stop*
Killing life without a knife.

**Jodie Warner (11)**
Elm Tree Middle School, Lowestoft

# A Greener Land!

What are we putting our world through
We are killing the Earth we belong to
We all pollute, you know it's true
There are things you know you shouldn't do

To make our lives better and care for us
There are plenty of things that cause no fuss
Recycle your bottles, papers and clothes
Simple things that everyone knows
Have smaller baths, turn down the light
All stick together to keep up the fight

Make everyone happy and lend a hand
To make a lasting greener land.

**Brodie Lock (12)**
Elm Tree Middle School, Lowestoft

# Poverty In Africa

How hungry I feel
My bones ache
All I ever wanted
Was a bit of cake
Maybe a grain of rice
It doesn't sound nice
I closed my eyes
And wished for a better place
When I woke up
Things were the same
Another day I shall lay
Till help comes my way.

**Savannah Capps (12)**
Elm Tree Middle School, Lowestoft

# Save The Earth

Turn off the light
and say goodnight
Turn off the light
and you'll be alright
Pick up that litter
I'm not being bitter
Please pick up that litter
Turn off the light
and say goodnight
Please turn off the light
and you'll be alright.

**Olivia Peat (12)**
Elm Tree Middle School, Lowestoft

## Think Of The People

Think of the people with nothing to eat,
Can't you donate that bit of meat?
When you look up at the stars tonight,
Think of the people who have no light.
When you wake up and bike to school,
You think life's bad, you must be a fool.
You get home from school and relax on your bed,
Think of the people that don't have a roof over their head.
For them every day is tougher,
But you think that you suffer.

**Jack Ellwood (11)**
Elm Tree Middle School, Lowestoft

## Help The World

Stop the famine
Stop the war
Help the people who are poor

Plant more trees
Drive cars less
Recycle more and leave less mess

Protect our planet
And don't delay
It's up to you, so start today.

**Christopher Jillings (11)**
Elm Tree Middle School, Lowestoft

# Recycling

R ecycling is kind for the environment,
E veryone should get involved and do their bit,
C ans, bottles and paper bins are available everywhere
Y ou can recycle a lot of useful materials,
C ars, tractors and lorries can also get recycled,
L ocal councillors do their bit,
I t's important to cut down the biggest problems at the landfill site,
N appies are one of the biggest problems at the landfill site,
G o and do your bit.

**Ebony Bond (11)**
Elm Tree Middle School, Lowestoft

# A Greener Life

Don't cut down the trees
Let's have a greener life
If we don't, we'll die

We don't have the rights to destroy the animals' home
Just to make us happy
Poisonous gas fills the air
It has to be clean
Just walk, don't go in a car.

**Steven Smallwood (11)**
Elm Tree Middle School, Lowestoft

# The Environment

Temperature is rising
Ice is melting
Down to global warming
We hear people calling.

Storms are raging
Animals are dying
Down to global warming
We hear people crying.

**Charlie Harrison-Reeve (11)**
Elm Tree Middle School, Lowestoft

# Recycling

Recycling is good for you,
You can help the planet too.
So start recycling now,
To help the environment.

Help us by doing your thing,
Recycle paper to help,
Recycle bottles to help,
Do this and help the planet.

**Katie Sadler (11)**
Elm Tree Middle School, Lowestoft

# Red Global Warming

Global warming
heed our warning
Destroying our planet
like an atomic bomb
Stop poverty
and hunger increasing numbers
The world would be a better place
if we stopped mankind's disgrace.

**Elenna Smither (11)**
Elm Tree Middle School, Lowestoft

# The Street Girl

Look at that girl on the street,
Go on give her a bite to eat or an umbrella, it's raining
You're all snuggled up, warm, not alone
Take a look at her, she is skin and bone, and alone
There's dangerous people out there,
Wouldn't you be scared if you were her?
Go on help her.

**Alice Edwards (11)**
Elm Tree Middle School, Lowestoft

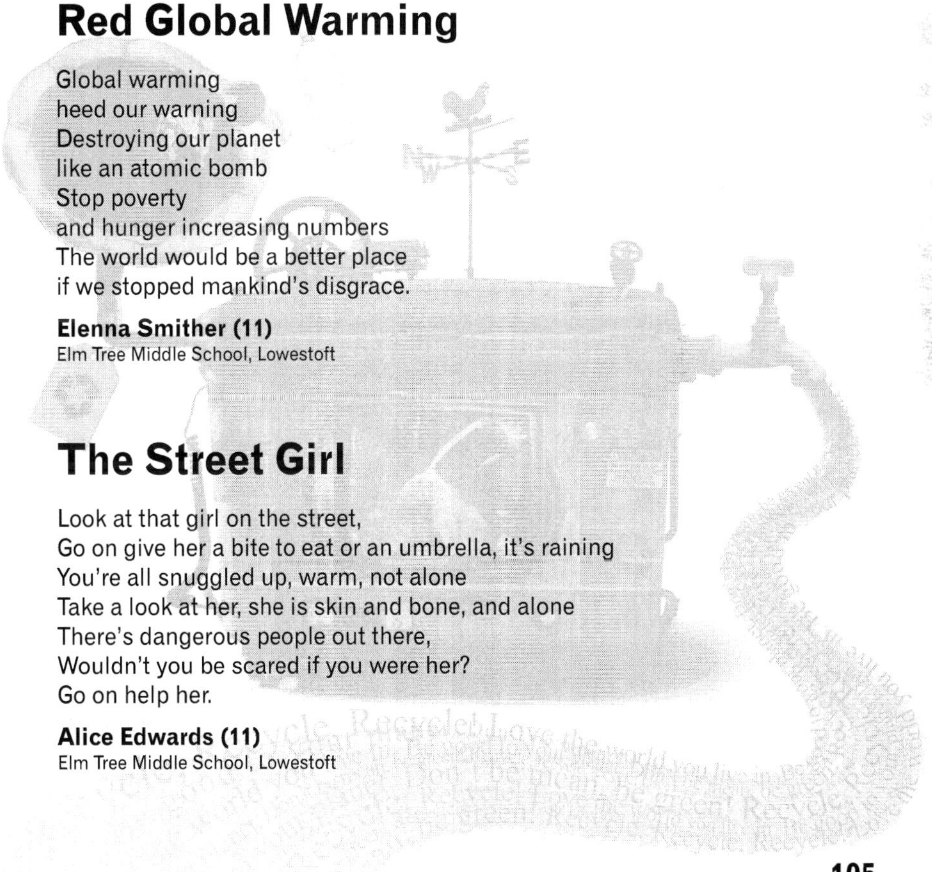

# Cars Kill Both Man And Earth

Don't travel by car, train or plane,
Cycle in the cycle lane,
Out with exhausts,
In with feet,
The pollution can make you ill,
Remember, cars can kill.

**Chantelle Cunningham (11)**
Elm Tree Middle School, Lowestoft

# At World's End

Look what we've done to the world today
Like nuclear radiation and extinction
Why do you fill your mind with climate change?
Action needs to be taken, not just thinking
Someone save our world.

**Connor Tooke (11)**
Elm Tree Middle School, Lowestoft

# Helping Poor Children

Why are so many people dying
at such a young age,
they need a good life too, just like us,
so please help them please!

**Nathan Bull (11)**
Elm Tree Middle School, Lowestoft

# Save The World

Don't melt the ice
If you do you've rolled the dice
By paying a big price
Then taking a slice of the environment.

**Jordan Johnston (11)**
Elm Tree Middle School, Lowestoft

# Recycle

Recycle your rubbish, don't just throw it away
It may come in handy some other day
You will never know that the rubbish that you throw
Could be your new jumper that your mum had to sew.

**Katherine Sewell (11)**
Elm Tree Middle School, Lowestoft

# Black And White

Does the colour of your skin matter?
Does it matter what nationality you are?
Why do you judge people?
And you wouldn't judge a car?

You give people names?
Because of their ethnicity,
But the real truth is
They're just like you and me
Black and white need to work together,
That's how it should be,
A piano would not sound,
Without black and white keys.

A classic game like chess,
Would be impossible to play,
If all the pieces were the same colour,
Which team would rule all the way?

Racism is very upsetting,
Why do people do it?
People shouldn't say such horrible things,
Not even a little bit!

**Richard Waterman (12)**
Northgate High School, Ipswich

# It's Me

Trees fall, birds call
every few minutes an animal loses its home
An animal dies, a human cries
the anger builds up inside me
A piece of paper in the bin
Why? When it's so easy to just put it in the blue bin

How I would love to step outside
and not see a single car
Just lots of people on bikes or walking
and smell the sweet smell of clean air.

An engine revs, a ton of $CO_2$
floats up making holes
you know where
Sudden heat, off drops some ice
a polar bear cries, its young dies
It's gone down deep.

It slowly melts
water floods down one by one
a country covered
We slowly freeze
a second ice age
it all starts again.

How I just wish
this world could be free
No tears, no death
no sadness, no worry.

It just makes me feel useless
like I can't do anything
like I want to take revenge
on those who cause this
But I know it's me . . .

**Katie Pettifor (12)**
Northgate High School, Ipswich

# De-Animal-Ation!

All things living in this world,
Are either living or dead,
Mostly animals,
Although we are animals,
Fighting for our lives,
There are creatures though,
That may lose theirs,

Like in the rainforest,
Trees gone down,
Spas up,
Heads down in favour,
But not for the animals,
For the people who build them,
*Deforestation!*

Like the poor orang-utan,
Hunted for its fur,
Bullets in,
Take aim,
Fire!
Skinned, eaten,
Rest sold,
To the butcher,
Who thinks it's beef,
Eaten by us,
Illegally smuggled,
It
Was
Just a poor defenceless,
Harmless, broken, orange
Animal.

**Ashley Jones (12)**
Northgate High School, Ipswich

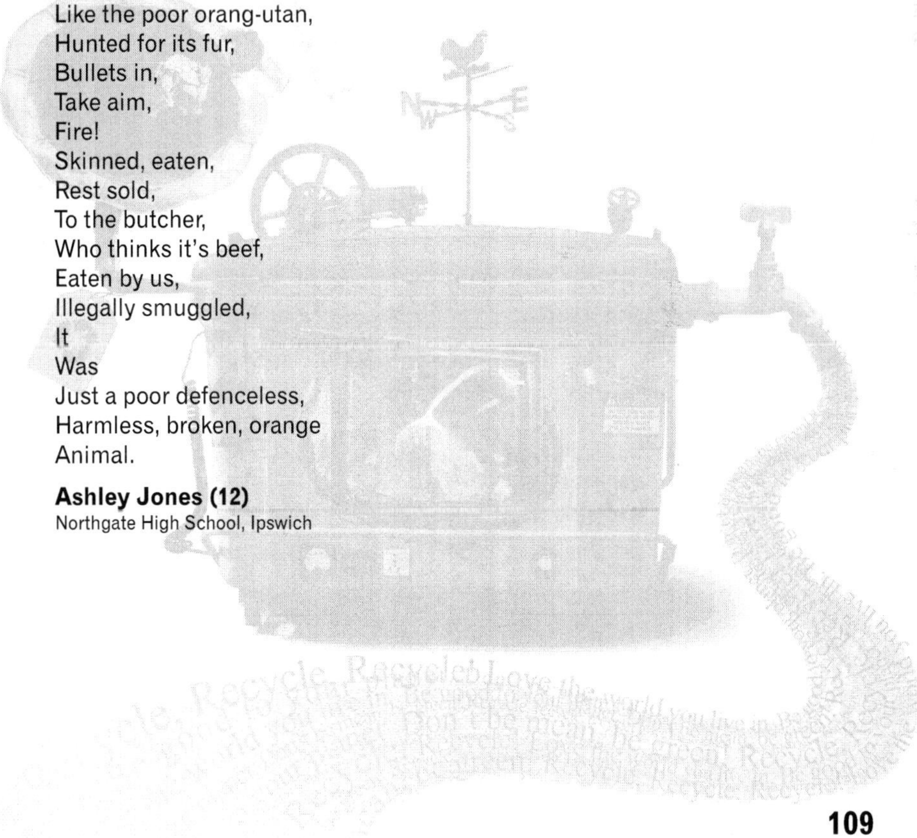

# The Backdrop Of Love

Love and hatred surrounds our lives on Earth,
The people we love will hate another,
Even the purest of people who live amongst us,
Can never be as pure as they believe,
For everyone will hate and most will love,
Together these things drive us mad,
To things we do not expect of,
Like murder and violence,
Cruelty and lies,
All for one we love,
If one knows of your love for them,
They may turn fickle and vain,
They will turn you down,
And feed off your sadness,
Maybe they'll just be playing,
But if they tell you to do things,
That you do not want to do,
For their love you will do anything
And lose your head in the end,
All for the one we love.

**Frederick Jago Farrow (13)**
Northgate High School, Ipswich

# On My Own

On my own,
I can't stop the hole expanding.
On my own,
I can't cage the violence.
On my own,
I can't stop the discrimination.
On my own,
I can't quench the greed.
On my own,
I can't stop the sorrow.
But together we will make a difference.

**Peter Smith (12)**
Northgate High School, Ipswich

# Save Us

Things that make me sad
Are turning the world bad
Like the credit crunch
Which sounds like some sort of brunch
The alcohol abuse
Which makes me pull a fuse
How we don't share the food
Whilst poor African countries starve, how rude
And smoking
People are choking
They won't make it to eighty
Trust me matey!
And in the Middle East shells are pelting

Everyone tries
But every six seconds a child dies
Pollution, save the planet
We have to help save and mean it
Every six seconds a mother cries.

**Elizabeth Asher (13)**
Northgate High School, Ipswich

# Save Them From Extinction

Extinction . . .
They're gone,
but we can save the rest.
We caused some deaths,
but we don't need to cause more.
Either dead by man or natural disasters,
save them.
They're helpless,
forest fires, earthquakes, hurricanes,
they're defenceless,
global warming, hunting and poachers.
They don't deserve this,
their life is rightfully theirs,
don't destroy them, it's unfair, save them . . .

**Hillary Lincoln (12)**
Northgate High School, Ipswich

# My World!

Do you want to grow up,
Living by machine,
Wishing you were younger,
Wishing you'd been more green?

Animals in extinction,
Just struggling to live.

Time has passed,
But we can still make a difference.
What should we do?
And to who should we give?

Stand up for your race,
And just be wise,
Give back the good respect
And don't worry about the prize.

**Juanita Richards (13)**
Northgate High School, Ipswich

# Racism

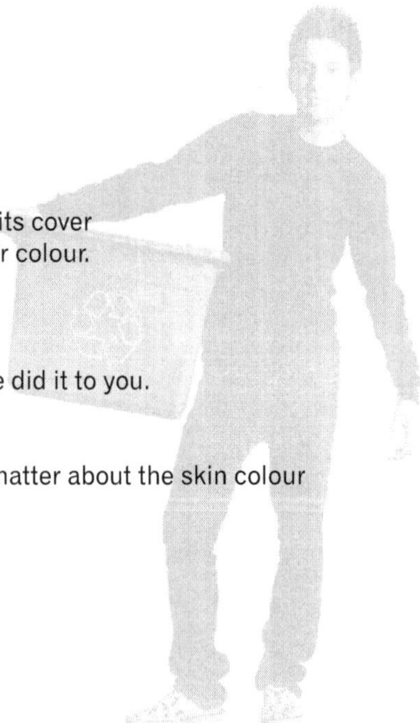

Don't do it,
Don't do it,
Don't do it,
You wouldn't judge a book by its cover
So why judge a person by their colour.
It's hurtful,
It's hurtful,
It's hurtful,
You wouldn't like it if someone did it to you.
It's annoying,
It's annoying,
People are people, it doesn't matter about the skin colour
So make it stop,
Stop,
Stop.

**Yasmin Williams (12)**
Northgate High School, Ipswich

## Help The World

Scientists are learning
that the sun won't be forever burning.
The winters are getting warmer
and the summers are getting colder
and the bright sun is getting older.
The stars are getting duller
and they're losing their pretty colour.
The ozone layer is breaking
parts of the Earth are shaking.
I am starting to worry.
We need to fix this mess in a hurry.

**Carlie Osborne (12)**
Northgate High School, Ipswich

## Poverty

Africa, America and Asia too
How to solve it, I wish I knew
People starving every day
'Cause they got no money to pay
No money to buy a comfy bed
No money to keep yourself fed
If only we all just gave a pound
The answer might just be found
So next time you see someone collecting money
Just give a bit it's not very funny.

**Tom Chamberlain (12)**
Northgate High School, Ipswich

# The Wonderful World

The wonderful world
ravaged around us
crushed about us
destroyed with us
vandalised about us
attacked around us
Killed
by
us
The wonderful world.

**Finn Rudkin (12)**
Northgate High School, Ipswich

# Pollution

The world is used as a rubbish bin,
With rubbish everywhere,
Chewing gum wrappers, crisp packets,
And no one seems to care,
When I'm walking down the street,
I get chewing gum stuck to my feet,
It makes me feel angry and annoyed,
That no one seems to care,
Where will this world end?
No one knows for sure!

**Jade Watson (12)**
Northgate High School, Ipswich

# Please Stop Pollution!

People driving their car,
Maybe not that far,
Doing lots of damage to the air,
People don't even seem to care,
This is the problem of pollution,
It's damaging the Earth,
It doesn't seem much now,
But it's causing the world to row.

**Aaron Sayer (13)**
Northgate High School, Ipswich

# Empty

You will be gone one day
But maybe not forever
If animals get extinct
You will regret it
The Earth will feel empty
I shall start to cry
Grey tears will fall upon us
Every day and night.

**Katya Banks (12)**
Northgate High School, Ipswich

# War - Haiku

In my home I hear
The explosions of missiles
Destroying the Earth.

**Marcus Rollins-Duvelle (12)**
Northgate High School, Ipswich

# Litter - Haiku

I'm a trash can, yeah
put your rubbish in me? Yeah
keep this world tidy.

**Daniel Powell (12)**
Northgate High School, Ipswich

# Respect The World

Across the fields of gold and green where cows graze and so do teens
Reading teeny magazines
Disrespecting Mother Nature
I'd like to put all men in danger
Respect the world and animals
They deserve to live in peace or their population will decrease
They become extinct some day
Try not to help them on their way.

**James Wear (13)**
Old Buckenham High School, Old Buckenham

# Untitled

What about air?
What about rain?
What about people living in a dream?
What about animals running?
How about love?
How about people living older and healthier?

Why do people live so bad?
How come people love the bad dirty world?
How do we live in toxic waste?
You give us clean water
We give you dirty water.

Where does the light come from?

**Ben Honeyball (11)**
Stowmarket Middle School, Stowmarket

# Re-Birth Earth!

The world today is falling to bits,
And if we are not careful,
We will all have to leave in spaceships.

All of us from around the world,
Let's get together and show our worth,
Let's work hard together,
And save our Earth.

Let's recycle our waste,
And save the Amazon,
Use less carbon,
Before it's all gone.

The ozone layer gets bigger each day,
Heating up our snow and ice,
Let's throw the CFCs away,
And to our Earth be nice.

Let's all work together, be a little cleaner,
Do away with our harmful ways,
Try and become a little greener,
Help the Earth, you know it pays.

Piece the world back together,
So our children can stay on Earth,
Look after the world we live in,
Let's give it a re-birth.

We are all responsible.

**Laura Cooper (12)**
Stowmarket Middle School, Stowmarket

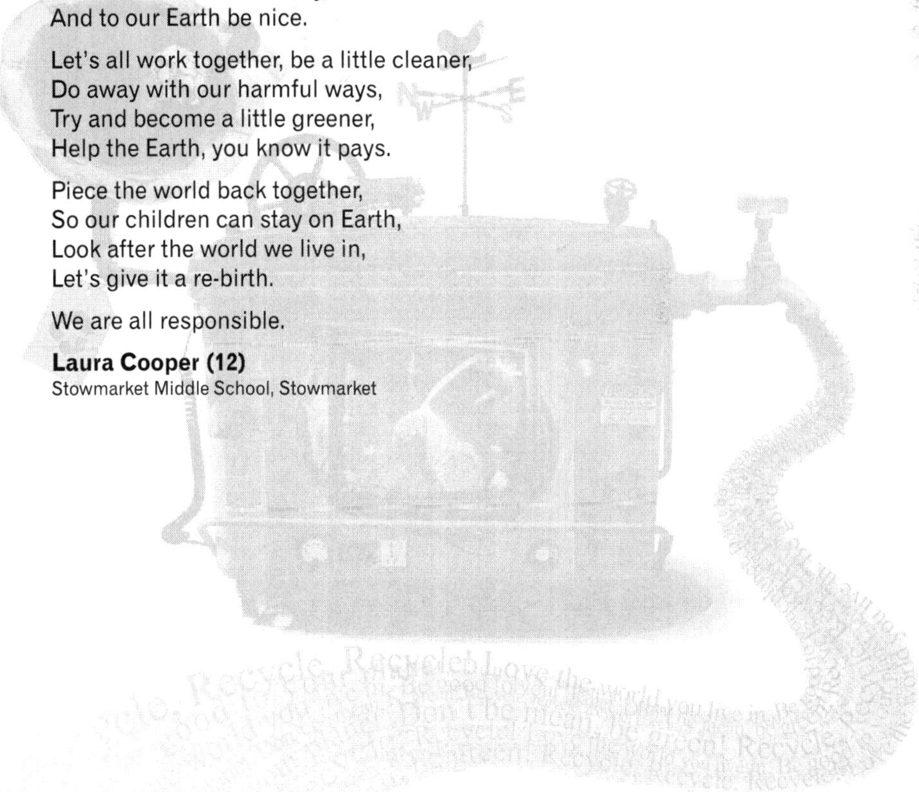

# Pollution/Extinction

Acid rain
Who's to blame?
Greenhouse effect
The thing we seem to respect
Pollution robs our air we breathe
Just because
We take more than we need

2008
A capacious mistake
The threat of extinction
Not enough volume

2010
Nothing by then
Gases and chemicals
Mixing in circles
Life gives us loads
Man gives back roads

2020
Our world near to empty
The climate reaching the end
No way Man can defend

2030
Land filthy, dirty
No animals, nor birds
No elephants in herds
A sound of a car
Hell so far

Acid rain
Who's to blame?
Greenhouse effect
The thing we seem to respect
Pollution robs our air we breathe
Just because
We take more than we need

By the year 2030
Around a quarter of all animals and birds will be extinct
Because of Man.

**Daisy Clarke (12)**
Stowmarket Middle School, Stowmarket

# Please Save It Now!

This is our planet,
We only have one,
I am only a child,
So what should be done?

Plastic bags are a major concern,
When will we ever learn!
All the other rubbish is just as bad,
It ruins all our land.

What are we doing?
We are ruining our world now,
All this can be changed,
But how?

*Reuse,*
*Reduce,*
*Recycle.*

So *reuse* what you can,
Then *recycle* at all times,
*Reduce* what's left,
And our world will be fine.

It's all our fault,
Our animals are fading fast,
A long distance memory, tigers and pandas?
How long will they last?

The world we are creating,
Was not the world we were given,
*Please save it now!*
While we are still living!

**Jordan Ayden (12)**
Stowmarket Middle School, Stowmarket

# We Hope Not

Global warming is coming,
you can feel it in the air.
The polar bears are dying,
because it's getting hot out there.
We try to recycle,
and we try to think green.
All of this to keep the world clean.

Homeless people lie on the streets,
without a thing to eat.
It's cold, it's wet, but people forget
how hard it is for them to survive.
They try to find shelter to stay alive.
They struggle on all alone,
it's no fault of their own.

It might seem good to cut down trees,
to get paper for writing and wood for building,
but without the trees and their green leaves,
we will not be able to breathe.
The rainforests help us out a lot,
so let's try our best to not cut them down.

What could happen in a few years?
Some people don't really care.
The animals could be dead,
because they were not aware what was ahead.
We all need to stop and think,
we all need to help out now,
before it becomes too late,
before the world turns into a terrible place.

**Sophie Reed (12)**
Stowmarket Middle School, Stowmarket

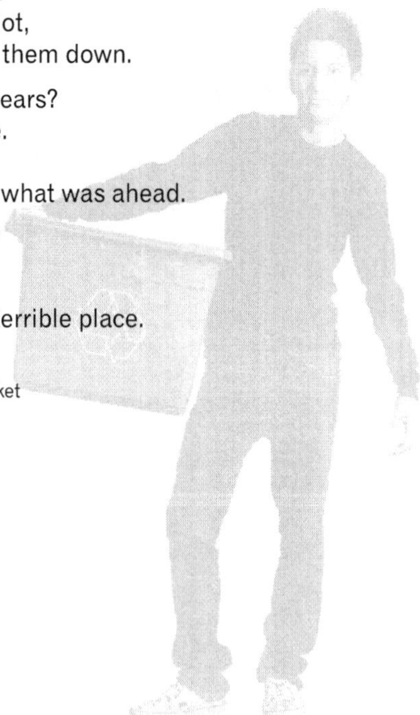

# I Made The World

I made the world,
Happy and bright,
What you are doing -
It isn't right.
I made the world,
Funny and sunny,
You turned it to power -
Turned it to money.
I gave you clean water,
To cook and to drink.
You polluted it -
Do you ever think?
I made the world,
With sweets and treats,
Coming in more and more,
But where's the packaging for all that food?
Where else?
But upon the floor,
When you drop litter,
I shout from the sky -
'Litterbug, litterbug, stop making Earth die!'
Yes. I'm the creator,
Master of Earth.
And I just gotta say -
*Stop littering my turf!*

**Toni-Leanne Hitch (12)**
Stowmarket Middle School, Stowmarket

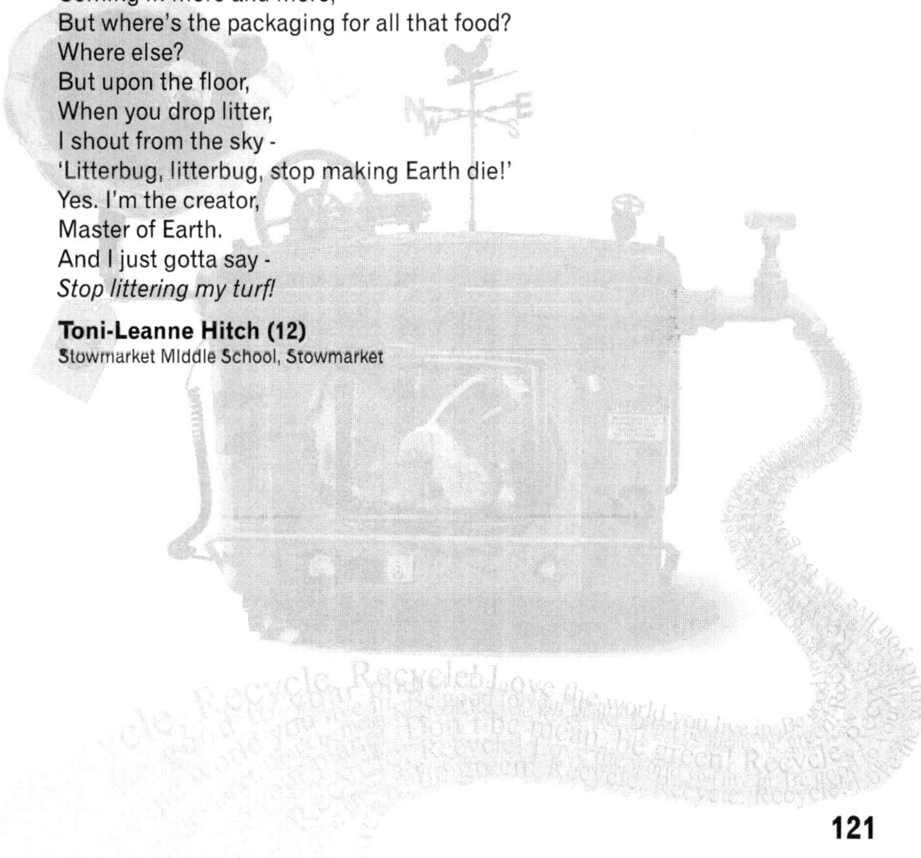

# Environmental Solution

Save our planet, we must all do more
Or it will be gone, you can be sure!

Exhaust fumes and too much pollution
Somebody help and find the solution.

Creatures extinct, wildlife dying
Trees falling down and nobody trying.

The ozone layer's wearing down
Pollution spreading closer to town.

Switch off lights when you leave
More oxygen will help us all to breathe.

Recycle your rubbish or use the bin
We'll beat the pollution and everyone wins.

Too much litter on the street
Rubbish and dirt beneath our feet.

Fields destroyed and habitats gone
Where did it all go so wrong?

The land will soon be covered in sea
Where will all the creatures be?

Save our planet, we must all do more
Or it will be gone you can be sure!

**Jane Hatchard (12)**
Stowmarket Middle School, Stowmarket

# Recycle, Recycle, Recycle

Recycling is good,
recycling is great,
recycling has nothing you could hate,
bottles, packets and wrappers,
put them in to recycle,
you can make a new bicycle.

Energy powers my lights,
energy powers my computer,
energy powers my telly
and saves it for the future.

Rubbish, rubbish, rubbish,
what are we going to do,
recycling helps for you, you and you.

Do you want the world to end,
the temperature is rising,
soon there will be no horizon.

Recycling is good for you,
recycling is good for me,
but think about it how difficult could it be.
Recycling is good,
recycling is great,
recycling has nothing you could hate.

**Megan Prentice (12)**
Stowmarket Middle School, Stowmarket

# Save Our World

Dogs are panting in the cars,
Humans smoking tonnes of tar,
Pollution making air unclean
And the sight of this is just obscene.

Trees disappearing day by day,
The Earth a mess by springtime May,
I know that we could stop all this,
No one listens, do I exist?

The lakes will soon shrivel up,
Which means we lost the ducks,
The ice caps will be nothing more,
Than the water on a market stall.

Every single thing will die out,
From the household mop to our crops,
Stop our selfishness think about,
Our lovely world, our habitat.

*Save our world,*
*Our home, our world!*

**Kim Allen (12)**
Stowmarket Middle School, Stowmarket

# Recycle, Recycle, Recycle

Recycle, recycle, recycle,
It's all you have to do,
Recycle, recycle, recycle,
It will include you.

Recycle, recycle, recycle,
It's not a hard thing to do,
Recycle, recycle, recycle,
So hurry up and do your part too.

Recycle, recycle, recycle,
If you want to help the world . . .

*Recycle, recycle, recycle!*

**Lois Maker (12)**
Stowmarket Middle School, Stowmarket

# Don't Take The Car To Work . . .

Don't take the car to work,
Don't take the car to school,
That should help the air get cleaner
And that will help us all.

Walk to work,
Walk to school,
It will help the environment
And that will help us all.

Think of all the trees that are being cut down,
Animals are losing their habitats,
Make sure you plant some more seeds for trees
And that will help us all.

So watch what you do
And remember to
Turn off your lights
And that will help us all.

**Alice Richmond (12)**
Stowmarket Middle School, Stowmarket

# When You Need Me

When you need me, I'm always there,
Even though you cut down my trees,
And although you never treat me with care,
When you need me, I'm always there.

When you need me, I'm always there,
Even though you pollute my seas,
And although you never treat me with care,
When you need me, I'm always there.

We are all linked together;
An invisible pact,
But what hurts me the most
Is a simple fact:

When you need me, I'm always there . . .
When I need you, you're never there.

**Ellen Butcher (13)**
Stowmarket Middle School, Stowmarket

# Reduce, Reuse, Recycle

Reduce, reuse, recycle,
three words everyone should know.
Reduce, reuse, recycle,
the way the world should go.

Reduce, reuse, recycle,
something everyone should do.
Reduce, reuse, recycle,
even your old shoe.

Reduce, reuse, recycle,
helps the world go round.
Reduce, reuse, recycle,
does not cost a pound.

Reduce, reuse, recycle,
you should all know how!
Reduce, reuse, recycle,
go and do it now.

**Abi Whitefield (12)**
Stowmarket Middle School, Stowmarket

# Save The World

Save the world,
Save the people,
Save the planet,
Save the trees,
Save the animals,
We don't want pollution,
We don't want extinction,
We don't want acid rain.
So as the fumes go in the air,
We must be aware,
We must take great care
And save the world.

**Kerri Rivers (12)**
Stowmarket Middle School, Stowmarket

# Big Green Poem

Cars, cars, everywhere,
Vroom vroom here,
Vroom vroom there,
Pumping fumes into the atmosphere.

Lorries here,
Lorries there,
Oil spills everywhere,
Driving through the thick smog,
Stopping people from having a jog.

Motorbikes here,
Motorbikes there,
Breathing hard, speeding fast,
Results in a crash, out on the scrapheap yard.

Beware, beware,
Pollution is everywhere.

**Zoë Smythe (13)**
Stowmarket Middle School, Stowmarket

# Untitled

The sun always rises,
We always leave our lights on.
The flowers always blossom,
We always graffiti with aerosol cans.
The trees always give us air,
We always cut the trees down.
We are always reproducing,
We are always building more houses.
The sea always gives us waves,
We always poison it.
We always moan that life isn't fair.
The Earth never complains.

**Miranda Messenger (12)**
Stowmarket Middle School, Stowmarket

# Untitled

You are missing your chance to live
And you will only get one chance
So be warned because I am not telling you again
So think fast.

When I give you fun and happiness
You give me sadness and grumpiness
So be quick before I blow up and that will be the end of you.

Your team of toil and poison have turned against you
So you are killing yourself as well.

So if you don't take your chance then that's the end of everything.

**Robbie Dickinson (11)**
Stowmarket Middle School, Stowmarket

# Process Of Paper

Men come with axes and chop down the trees,
To help pay their taxes and for expensive things,
Homes of animals, plants, insects and bees, destroyed for money, they're not thinking of these,
Making money for families,
Bringing logs to factories,
Constructing paper using awful machines,
Creating pollution and paper for me,
Even this paper was made by trees,
So use both sides and recycle your paper,
But don't reuse your toilet paper.

**Megan Cocksedge (12)**
Stowmarket Middle School, Stowmarket

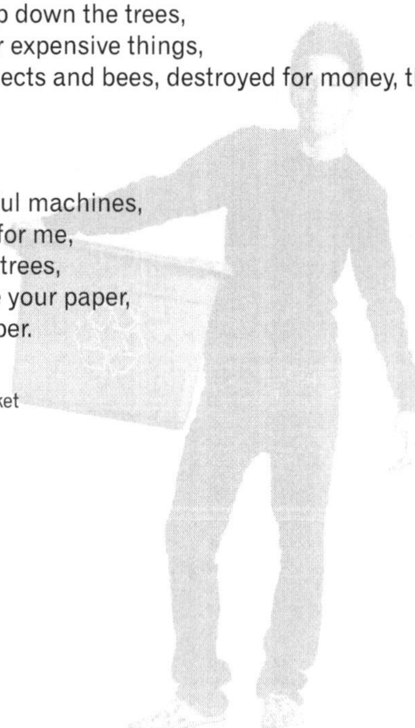

# The Things That We Do

We make poisonous gases fill the air,
We are endangering the panda bear.

Pure snow on the mountaintops,
We make acid raindrops.

In the jungle there are wild boar,
While we are declaring war.

The world gives us so much,
But we destroy the world.

We need to change.

**Lucy Jennings (12)**
Stowmarket Middle School, Stowmarket

# Can We Find What We Have Lost?

Don't drive a car,
Your contribution will go far.
Motorbikes go quick,
But they won't help us fix,
The damage we have caused.
A bicycle is good,
You really, really should,
Ride it to and from.
You can switch a light on and off,
But you can't regain what we have lost!

**Eve-Marie Randall (13)**
Stowmarket Middle School, Stowmarket

# The Earth Gives Us

The Earth gives us snow,
We give back acid rain,
The Earth gives us air,
We give back poison,
The Earth gives us trees,
We give back rubbish dumps,
The Earth gives us natural beauty,
We give back graffiti,
The Earth gives us peace,
We gave back war.

**Ellen Thoroughgood (12)**
Stowmarket Middle School, Stowmarket

# Help Save The World

R ecycling saves resources
E verything you recycle helps the world
C ans, bottles, newspapers, can be recycled
Y ou can help make a difference
C ardboard, plastic, carrier bags and containers
L osers don't recycle
E arth is our home, keep it clean.

**Miranda Stark (12)**
Stowmarket Middle School, Stowmarket

# Young Writers Information

We hope you have enjoyed reading this book - and that you will continue to enjoy it in the coming years.

If you like reading and writing poetry drop us a line, or give us a call, and we'll send you a free information pack.

Alternatively if you would like to order further copies of this book or any of our other titles, then please give us a call or log onto our website at www.youngwriters.co.uk

Young Writers Information
Remus House
Coltsfoot Drive
Peterborough
PE2 9JX
(01733) 890066